THE ISRAEL EXPERIENCE BOOK

D0238922

David Breakstone
& Cindy Jochnowitz

BLOCH PUBLISHING COMPANY
New York

Library of Congress Catalogue Card Number 76-56985

ISBN 0-8197-0021-5

Grateful appreciation is extended to those who granted permission to reprint quotations from their respective publications, appearing in this volume on the pages noted: pp.47-48, to Muki Tsur, for material excerpted from **What is Kibbutz?**, published by The Federation of Kibbutzim in Israel, 1972; p.62, to the World Zionist Organization, for the excerpt from Yitzchak Rabin's *Address at a Hebrew University Graduation Ceremony*, reprinted in their publication **In the Dispersion**, vol. 7, no. 10, 1967; pp.65-66, from **The Jewish War** by Josephus. Translated by G.A. Williamson. Reprinted by permission of Viking Books Ltd., publishers; pp.69-70. to A.S. Barnes & Company, Inc., for the quotations from **Herzl's Diaries**, Thomas Yoseloff, publisher; pp.69, 125, 139, 251, to The Jewish Publication Society of America for the quotations from Herzl's *Address to the First Zionist Congress*, Ben-Gurion's *The Imperatives of the Jewish Revolution*, and A.D. Gordon's *Logic for the Future*, excerpted from **The Zionist Idea** edited by Arthur Hertzberg, published by the JPS in 1959 and now available in an Atheneum edition; p.74, to ACUM, Ltd., for permission to reprint from the diaries and letters of Yosef Trumpeldor, appearing in **Zichronot Eretz Yisrael** by Avraham Yaari. Translated and abridged by Israel Schen under the title **The Godly Heritage**, published by the Youth and Hechalutz Department of the Zionist Organization, 1958; pp.80-81 (first quotation) and p.107, from **The Gates of the Forest** by Elie Wiesel. Translated by Frances Frenaye. Copyright © 1966 by Holt, Rinehart and Winston. Reprinted by permission of Holt, Rinehart and Winston, Publishers; p.81 (second quotation), reprinted by the permission of Farrar, Straus & Giroux, Inc. from **Night** by Elie Wiesel, copyright © 1960 by MacGibbon & Kee; originally published in French by Les Editions de Minuit, © 1958; p.81 (third quotation) from **The Town Beyond the Wall** by Elie Wiesel. Reprinted by permission of Holt, Rinehart and Winston, Publishers; pp.81-82, from **Anne Frank: The Diary of a Young Girl** by Anne Frank, copyright 1952 by Otto Frank. Reprinted by permission of Doubleday & Company, Inc.; p.83, to Bloch Publishing Company for the quotation by Eric A. Kimmel, excerpted from **Living After the Holocaust** edited by Lucy Y. Steinitz and David M. Szonyi; pp.84, 165, 249, to ACUM, Ltd., for permission to reprint the songs appearing on those pages, and to the Youth and Hechalutz Department of the World Zionist Organization for permission to reprint their English translations of the songs appearing on pages 124, 165, and 249; p.89, to Hadar Publishing House Ltd. for permission to reprint Dov Gruner's letter appearing in **The Conquest of the Acre Fortress** by Jan Gitlin, © 1974 by Hadar Publishing House; p.101, to Bloch Publishing Company for the quotation from the **Daily Prayer Book** edited by Dr. Joseph Hertz, copyright 1948 by Ruth Hecht; p.102, *i thank you* copyright 1947 by E.E. Cummings, copyright 1975, by Nancy T. Andrews. Reprinted by permission of Harcourt Brace Jovanovich, Inc.; p.102, Hassidic saying reprinted by permission of Schocken Books, Inc., from **Ten Rungs: Hassidic Sayings** edited by Martin Buber, copyright © 1947 by Schocken Books, Inc. Copyright renewed © 1975 by Schocken Books, Inc.; p.104, to Media Judaica Inc. for permission to reprint the poem by Aaron Zeitlin appearing in **New Prayers for the High Holy Days** edited by Rabbi Jack Riemer; pp.105, 106, 107, 120, the quotations from A.J. Heschel are reprinted with the permission of Farrar, Straus & Giroux, Inc. from **Israel: An Echo of Eternity** by Abraham Joshua Heschel, copyright © 1967, 1968, 1969, by Abraham Joshua Heschel; pp.109, 113, the quotations from A.J. Heschel are reprinted with the permission of Farrar, Straus, & Giroux, Inc. from **The Sabbath** by Abraham Joshua Heschel, copyright 1951 by Abraham Joshua Heschel. All rights reserved; p.112, from **You Shall Be As Gods** by Erich Fromm. Copyright © 1966 by Erich Fromm. Reprinted by permission of Holt, Rinehart and Winston, Publishers; p.124, to Chappell Music Company, for permission to reprint excerpts from *Jerusalem of Gold* © Naomi Shemer; p.132, from p.230 of the book **And the Hills Shouted for Joy** by Bernard Postal and Henry W. Levy. copyright © 1973. Published by David McKay Company, Inc. Reprinted by permission of the publisher; the English translations of the Bible are from the edition of **The Holy Scriptures** published by The Jewish Publication Society of America, © 1947, 1945, except in a few instances where the translations are those of the authors.

Designed at the Israel Economist, Jerusalem (02) 234131

Illustrated by Lika Tov, Graphic design by Shelley Schwartz

Bloch Publishing Company, Inc.

Printed in the United States of America

Dedication

TO LITA SMITH, whose intimate involvement in the evolution of our commitment to Israel makes her a friend forever — even though she never writes!

Appreciation

THE CENTER FOR JEWISH EDUCATION IN THE DIASPORA of Hebrew University extended support and cooperation in the production of an earlier experimental edition of this book which permitted the current volume to become a reality.

Inspiration

ON THE COVER — We find ourselves today in an unfinished Israel, not only whose physical borders are still to be set, but whose social fabric, cultural composition, and spiritual meaning are yet to be consciously evolved. It is for each individual to determine his or her own relationship to the effort.

Hesitation

WARNING — Use of this book may be dangerous if not accompanied by appropriate dosages of: 1) a **regular** guide to Israel, 2) the Bible and a prayerbook, and 3) discussion with friends. **Proceed accordingly.**

Acknowledgements

> One who learns from his friend ... ought to pay him honor
> -Parke Avot

react

We extend a special thank you to Dr. Barry Chazan and Dr. Michael Rosenak whose personal concern with us and our endeavors deeply influenced the preparation of this book, and who, as members of the faculty of The Center for Jewish Education in the Diaspora of The Hebrew University of Jerusalem, greatly facilitated this publication. Their advice, if not consistently heeded, is always cherished.

We also thank Cathy Berger, Robert Brack, David Goldman, Lesley Loke, Marlen Mertz, Janie Taff-Shukrun, and Momi Shukrun who provided moral support and technical assistance above and beyond the call of friendship. They didn't always know what they were getting into; sometimes they just stopped in for coffee at the wrong time. But they kept coming back.

And we are grateful to Alan Bennett and Yaakov Reshef. This book is a partial reflection of the inspiration they gave us to build upon many of their dreams.

We also want to acknowledge Rabbi Gilbert Rosenthal, Bob Ross-Tabak, Rabbi Benamin Siegal, Susan and Ozzie Teller, and the American Zionist Youth Foundation, the Hadassah Zionist Youth Commission, and the Youth and Hechalutz Department of the World Zionist Organization who helped us in bringing the manuscript passed one stage or another, one way or another.

We are likewise indebted to the many Israel summer program participants who served as our highly esteemed guinea pigs for the early experimental editions of this book. We have done our best to incorporate their valuable suggestions.

And of course we want to mention the assistance received from Charles Bloch, Lisa Besdin and David Szonyi of Bloch Publishing Company, Inc. whose comments and efforts were of inestimable value to us in bringing the final draft of this book to its present state.

And finally, needless to say, we appreciate Our parents who, because of the values they instilled in us, are largely responsible for our being in Israel at all. They're still trying to figure out where they went wrong! They didn't.

comment

If there be others whom we have forgotten to mention, we apologize; and if they indeed be our friends, they will forgive us — We hope!

Furthermore, despite all the assistance mentioned above, this book will certainly have its shortcomings. For them, we can credit only ourselves.

Finally, we are most anxious to receive comments from you — They will help us immeasurably in preparing future editions of this book. Please contact us either through Bloch Publishing Company, New York, or directly at Neve Ilan, D.N. Harei Yehuda, Israel.

TABLE OF CONTENTS

שלום
Shalom

A Personal Introduction

Israel is more than its number of square miles. It's a concept as well, rich in history, philosophy, and life style. It's a tiny nation struggling for meaningful survival in the midst of enemies sworn to its destruction . . .

Big deal.

Well, actually it is a big deal. But you've heard all that already. Does it mean anything?

Israel has problems. Have you heard that? And all kinds too. Not all the Arabs and Jews get along. Not even the kids. The religious and non-religious often disagree. Sometimes violently. The Jews of Middle Eastern and North African origin often suffer from social prejudices held against them by some Western Jews and Sabras. Israelis push, yell, hustle, demand, and sneer. They're plain arrogant at times.

People ask us, then, if we're here for good. We wonder; for good? It's not as simple as all that, because for good or for bad, we're here to stay. Born and bred in America, we've discovered that for us Israel is home. There are a lot of things involved, like . . .

AbrahamEgyptExodusSinaiFirstTempleProphetsKings586BCE
Tishab'AvExileGalutSecondTemple70CEMassadaTalmudCrusa
desSpanishInquisitionEuropePogromsEmancipationEnlightenm
entBiluimDreyfusHerzlGhettoBalfourDeclarationChalutzimSec
ondAliyaKibbutzHolocaustWhitePaperBenGurion1947SixDay
WarYomKippurWarUNEntebbe . . .

They comprise only a small part of what our Israel is all about; and with everything that ties them together, though they don't do away with the problems mentioned above, they do explain them a little.

We'll lay it on the line. We're in love with Israel. And we'd like you to share that love with us; we're not hiding that. But if you think this place is going to be perfect, forget it. And if you expect to find that everyone here is one of those "beautiful people," you're undoubtedly going to be more than disappointed.

Understand, there's this thing called Zionism. It's complex, but basically it's an ideology that says Jews can only be really full people if they have the opportunity to work and create on their own land. Being employed by others or being only employers isn't basic enough. It keeps a people from developing its own way of doing things. Self-determination. Self-expression. Who am I? What am I? Why am I? Israel challenges us: stop only asking how. Do what's you, where it's you, and find out. Zionism.

The land of Israel is called life.
-Talmud

For us, what it means is this: Israel, the Jews, and Jewish history are all tied together forever. The Land, the People, and the Book. *Eretz Yisrael* (ארץ ישראל) *Am Yisrael* (עם ישראל) and *Torat Yisrael* (תורת ישראל). They're inseparable. They grew together, and it's unnatural — and impossible — to keep them apart. So much of what it is that is Jewish — the traditions, the customs, the holidays, the celebrations, the rituals, the values, the symbols — combine all three, and are rooted in their interrelation. But an introduction like this can't explain how. That's a process we leave to you and the time you're here.

And as the interaction continues, maybe you'll begin to love Israel too. Not because you'll have had a great time (though no doubt you will), but because Israel is not Europe, or any place else you might have chosen for a vacation. Israel is Israel. And maybe you will begin to feel you belong here. Maybe not. But at least you will start to understand why others feel they do. Because luxuries aren't as important to them as are basics: a place to call home, you, and your roots. There it is again: Land, People, and Book.

The relationship we're talking about takes on meaning only as the individual begins to figure out the triangle. Facts, ideology, ideas — they're all important, but only inasmuch as they help provide a perspective from which to view oneself in context of the Jewish world.

Should we say it more simply? Being in Israel only makes sense if it helps make sense out of being Jewish.

It has for us. We've written this book with the hope that it also will for you.

David & Cindy

Neve Ilan, 5737 (1977)

Section 1
PRE-DEPARTURE

This Book:

What It Is...

We don't know how to classify this book. We know what it is, we just don't know what to call it. For convenience sake, we'll say it's a guide to Israel. But actually it's a guide to you. To you *and* Israel, in fact. To your relationship. *L'chaim*!

And we have another problem. We don't know exactly how to explain who the book is for. Young people probably, who are in Israel for a summer vacation, for a stay on kibbutz, or for a year of study and travel. For students who are learning about Israel anywhere, with, perhaps, a visit to the Jewish State in mind. And for older folks as well, doing any of these same things, who can still think like young people, and who can enjoy what young people enjoy.

But what's most important of all, is that this book is for those who want to bring more back from Israel than pictures, who want to be more than just another tourist in the Holy Land, who feel they haven't gotten their money's worth until they've gotten their "meaning's worth." We don't suggest you leave the camera and guidebook behind, but what we've put together here also demands some hard thinking about how you personally connect to all that is going on around you — and a pen with which to work it all out.

We've attempted to supply the tools and the inspiration necessary for you to explore the Israel of the Israelis, and to encourage you to take stock of yourself as a Diaspora Jew now in your homeland. But the leg work must be your own, and so too the discoveries.

... And How To Use It

We're not intent here on having you memorize facts, nor are we concerned with influencing you towards the acceptance of any particular ideology (though we've supplied some of each). And least of all do we want our experiences to serve as substitute for your own. Therefore:

browse Familiarize yourself with the book. Simply looking through its pages, and finding whatever you may (or may not) be looking for, is probably the best way of getting to know what's in it. Then, while exploring Israel on your own, you'll have a good idea of just how this "manual" can be of most use to you, personally.

scribble There's a lot of empty space in this book. It's yours. Use it for keeping track of your thoughts and exploits. Organize and immortalize them. It's always fun to look back later on what you once felt. Don't, however, feel stifled by the structures we've provided. They're meant to stimulate, not constrict, your thinking. Use our fill-ins if they're right for you; skip them if they're not. We won't be insulted if you do things your own way.

share Broaden your horizons. Everyone comes away from Israel with revelations of their own. Discuss your reactions with others. Sharing adventures is an adventure itself.

prepare Don't wait until you leave Israel to use this book. Look over the sections about places and cities before you get to them. Refer to them while you're visiting. And review them afterwards, adding your own comments — and the things we missed. Use other entries in a similar way, whatever aspect of Israel you're exploring.

remember This book has several "re-usable" sections: places to keep track of every Shabbat, to note the contrasts you see around you, to record the archaeological sites you visit, and so on; lists of Biblical passages naming places in Israel, of useful addresses for all sorts of things, of Hebrew words helpful for getting around, of historical events to keep things in perspective, etc. Find them, and don't abandon them.

reflect We've left a whole section blank. Don't you leave it the same way.

relate Talk to this book. Feed it. Give it a name. Make it your own. Show it concern. We expect it will respond.

Preconceived Notions

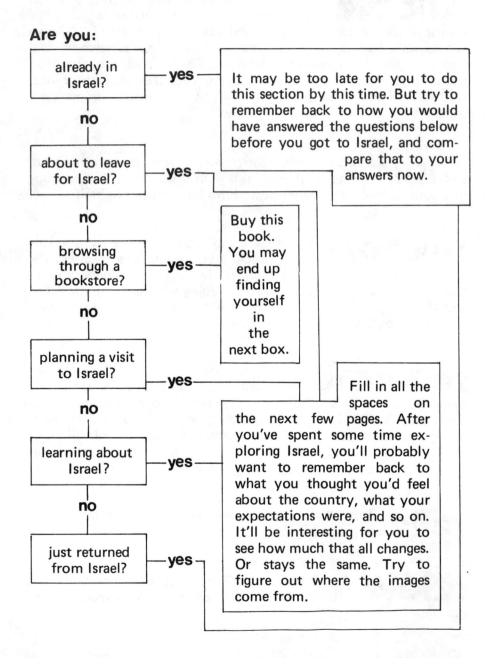

Are you:

already in Israel? — **yes** — It may be too late for you to do this section by this time. But try to remember back to how you would have answered the questions below before you got to Israel, and compare that to your answers now.

no

about to leave for Israel? — **yes**

no

browsing through a bookstore? — **yes** — Buy this book. You may end up finding yourself in the next box.

no

planning a visit to Israel? — **yes**

Fill in all the spaces on the next few pages. After you've spent some time exploring Israel, you'll probably want to remember back to what you thought you'd feel about the country, what your expectations were, and so on. It'll be interesting for you to see how much that all changes. Or stays the same. Try to figure out where the images come from.

no

learning about Israel? — **yes**

no

just returned from Israel? — **yes**

NOW THEN

1) How do you feel about being Jewish? and everything around you being Jewish?

tomatoes and cucumbers for breakfast? and tomatoes and cucumbers for dinner?

speaking Hebrew? and not understanding everyone else's Hebrew?

being a citizen of the country you're from? and living in Israel?

camels and sheep being a part of everyday life? and swimming in the Mediterranean?

seeing borders of Arab countries up close? and Arabs and Jews living together?

taking long hikes through the countryside? and getting up at 4 a.m. to take long hikes through the countryside?

being alongside the grave of Abraham? and walking through 2000 year old cities and buildings?

2) What are your expectations of Israel in general?

3) And specifically — How many people live in Israel? . . . .
Are they all Jews? If not, who are the others, and how many are
there? . . . .
Where do all the people come from? . . . .
. . . .
How many channels does Israeli TV have? . . . . . . What percentage
of Israelis are religious? . . . . What percentage of Israelis live
on kibbutz? . . . . What percentage of Israelis go into the army? . . . .
What percentage of Israelis are always right? . . . . What is
felafel? . . . . How much of Israel is desert? . . . .
How often does it rain between April and October? . . . .

4) What would you like to find in Israel?

5) And why are you going, anyway?

6) Now forget about this for a while. That's important. Try to
experience Israel fresh. Don't force the country or its people into
any mold once you're there. Trying to make everything fit will turn
Israel and its inhabitants into stereotypes, denying you the possibility of evolving any sort of honest relationship with the Jewish
State. And that, as we've said, is what we're really concerned about.
Be flexible and open-minded. Don't think of Israelis as being just like
the people where you're from, only brought up in a foreign country
and speaking a foreign language. They're not. They've developed
their own way of doing things, and they're not the ways you're used
to. But just what they are, is for you to discover yourself. Enjoy!

Section 2

EVERYTHING
ISRAEL

Off The Beaten Path

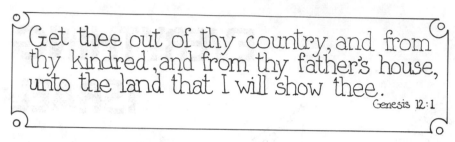

Get thee out of thy country, and from thy kindred, and from thy father's house, unto the land that I will show thee.

Genesis 12:1

Some suggestions for things to do during your free time, or, if you're with a group, to tell your counsellor (מדריך/ה) *you have to do if you want to go off on your own. Fill up the spaces between the ideas with what happens, but don't be satisfied with your experiences only. Ask friends about theirs. How much of it meshes with the life you're used to?*

1. Take any bus to the end of the line and explore.

2. Go into a supermarket or *makolet* (מכולת) — a what! ? — and see how much it would cost for a good meal. Do you know what it would cost where you come from? Go into a clothing store and see if you can afford a new pair of jeans.

3. The next time you pass by a beggar, think for a minute. Try to find out what Maimonides would have you do. (Hint: He once said: *"Nobody is ever impoverished through the giving of charity."*)

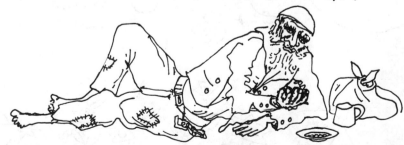

10

4. Go to an outdoor market. Mingle with the crowd and the smells. Compare prices with the stores. Watch the Israelis bargain. Try it yourself if you want to buy something. (The Talmud tells us not to even start bargaining unless we're seriously intending to buy.)

5. Visit a university campus and compare what you see there to what you'd expect to find, or already know about, on a college campus back where you come from. How old are the students? What did they do before college?

6. Go into Mea She'arim (find it on a map of Jerusalem) and compare its streets, houses, and standard of living to those of the Old City or Rehaviya (also on the Jerusalem map). Who lives where and what are the differences?

7. If someone invites you for *aruchat arba* (ארוחת ארבע)   don't say *gezundheit*. Go, listen, absorb, ask, eat.

8. Talk to some Israelis your own age. Ask about the things they do in a normal day. How do they feel about the army?

9. Buy a newspaper (the *Jerusalem Post* is in English.) Read about what's going on around you. See how the Israelis report the daily situation in Israel and the world. Read some foreign press and compare coverage of the same events.

10. Listen for the *beep . . . beep . . . beep* that comes over the radio before the news broadcast every hour. If you can't understand anything, just watch the faces of the people around you — especially if you're on a public bus.

11. Have an *ice-cafe* some time when you're tired and thirsty. Trust us.

12. Try to stand on line to get on a bus some Friday afternoon without pushing. Don't bother trying too long.

13. Try to cash a traveler's check in less than half an hour.

14. Notice the things around you. Try to take pictures with your mind as well as with your camera.

Scramble

Decipher the names of these fruits, all grown in Israel. Unjumble the letters of each word below, and write them correctly in the spaces provided.

R E A P R G U T I F _ _(_)_ _(_)_ _ _ _
(one of Israel's major exports)

S O L E V I _(_)_ _(_)_
(the branch they grow on has been a symbol of peace since the time of the Bible)

F S I G (_)_ _ _
(outside Israel you've probably only seen them dried, brown, and flat)

S P E R A G _ _ _ _(_)_
(prepared one way, they get you drunk)

P S E L A P _ _ _(_)_ _
(Eve may have done the tempting, but Adam ate one out of his own lack of willpower)

Next, correctly combine the circled letters of each word you've formed, and come up with another Israeli food -- one you can snack on the next time you're out exploring: _ _ _ _ _ _ _

For those who are hungrier than they are interested in playing our game, the answers appear on page 245.)

A Menorah Plant?[1]

 The official emblem of the State of Israel is a menorah embraced by two olive branches. To understand its origins is to appreciate the concept of a contemporary Jewry rooted in its ancient Hebrew culture. That might sound a bit heavy, but what it means is this: The idea behind building a Jewish State is nothing new; it's based on something the Jewish people already had thousands of years ago.

Read chapter 4, verses 1-14 in the book of the prophet Zechariah. Until you get around to it, what it basically says is this:

After the destruction of the First Temple   (בית ראשון)   (586 BC) and the subsequent exile to Babylonia, the Jews finally made their way back to *Eretz Yisrael*. They started to rebuild the Temple in Jerusalem, but the work — which was extremely difficult to begin with — was not made any easier by the fact that surrounding enemies kept attacking. Eventually the people became overwhelmed and gave up altogether. But God's plans called for something more, we are told, and he arranged for Zechariah to experience a dream or a vision. In it he saw a huge menorah with a strong olive tree standing on either side of it. After assuring an angel that he really had no idea what this whole thing was all about, he was helped to see things he hadn't before noticed.

In the seven flames of the menorah he was able to read the words, *"Lo b'chayal v'lo b'koach ki im-b'ruchi*   (לא בחיל ולא בכח כי אם ברוחי)— Neither by might, nor by power but by My spirit," and in the two trees he was able to recognize Joshua (Israel's high priest at the time) and Zerubabel (the governor). Is the message clear?

This dream, which Zechariah used to inspire the people to continue in their work on the Temple, is as important to us today as it was over 2000 years ago to our ancestors. Those who are building today's Israel also have to rebuild the country with the spirit of righteousness and not of war, and all types of leaders and people must embrace the task together if the attacking enemies are indeed to be held back.

As to where the symbol originally came from, take a look at the picture. Looks kind of like a menorah, doesn't it? Read Exodus 25:31-32. That's the first time a menorah is mentioned in the Bible. Notice all the botanical terms. The design is probably based on the *moriah* plant (picture). That doesn't mean the Jews worshipped plants or the physical world, but it does seem to indicate that nature was a fairly common reference point for the Jewish people in the evolution of their symbols and traditions.

The story behind the olive tree (the other part of our symbol) suggests the same thing. Remember what the dove finally brought back to Noah (Genesis 8:11)? Or look at Exodus 27:20. Did you know that the explanation behind what's written there is that olive oil gives off the steadiest and brightest of all natural flames, so the Rabbis said it alone was suitable as a "light unto the nations?" Also, notice some time what a grove of olive trees looks like fluttering in the wind and sun. That wave-of-light effect comes from the silvery sheen on the underside of the olive leaf. And finally, the olive tree is an especially sturdy model, able to undergo many hardships and able to live for centuries, unlike many other species in the Middle East. The early Hebrew associations with it as a symbol of peace, light, and endurance are certainly understandable.

In quick summary, then, what we've got is this: the ancient tradition of rebuilding the Temple, the spiritual value of peace preferred to war, and the living symbols of the *moriah* plant and the olive tree. Only in the context of *Eretz Yisrael* can the Jewish nation translate into deed this inspiration from our sources. The Land, the People, and the Book.

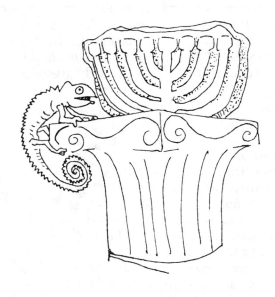

The Everything Israel

You might want to do this puzzle together with a few other people. If you still can't come up with all the answers, you can find them on p.245. But if you do look them up, be sure that you at least learn something in the process!

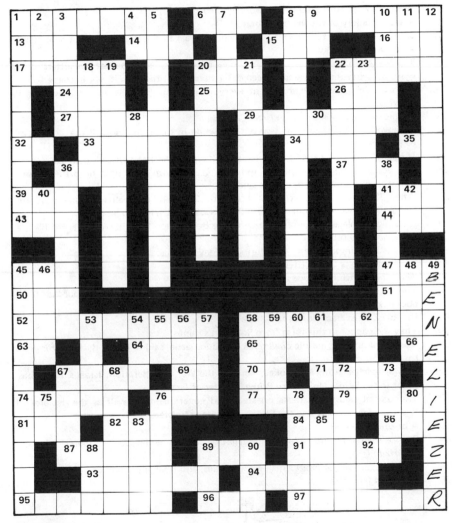

them on p.245.

ACROSS

1.   They say it won't fall again; symbol of Jewish resistance.

6.   _ _ _*Kinneret* (sea, in Heb.); sweet potato in Eng.

8.   Heb. for village or rural settlement.

13. My God (Heb.); Hebrew name.
14. Jewish women's organization dedicated to fund-raising and vocational training.
15. *"Lo yisa ___ el ___ cherev."*
16. Fourth book of the Bible (Eng. abbrev.)
17. Book of Biblical love poetry using nature as its motif, some say describing the relationship of God to the Jewish people. Song of _____
20. *"___ by might nor by power but by My spirit."* (Zech. 4:6) The faith with which Jews 2000 years ago and again today returned to rebuild the Jewish homeland.
22. A pressing concern of the world Jewish community today is the fate of Soviet _____.
24. Association of Antiquated Educators (abbrev.)*
25. African Society of Elephants (abbrev.)*
26. Jews have longed to return to the Land of Israel in every ___; also, Equal Rights Amendment (abbrev.)
27. Teachers keep trying to _____ ideas in students; also, the last five letters of the word tell what the people have been doing here to get their land back in shape.
29. An essential personage present at every meaningful Bar Mitzvah and wedding in America!
32. People or nation (Heb.); ___ *Yisrael Chai!*
33. In Jewish tradition you don't wear them while in mourning; also, if the _____ fits, wear it.
34. It might be said that the State of Israel itself was David Ben-Gurion's greatest.
35. The Jewish people are supposed to be an *"__ l'goyim"* — a light unto the nations; also, the olive branch is one of its symbols.
36. When 33 nations said it at the U.N. on Nov. 29, 1947, the reality of what *chalutzim* (חלוצים) had been building for 50 years was officially recognized.
37. ___ Boker, Negev kibbutz and oasis where Ben-Gurion lived the last years of his life.
39. with me (in Heb.)
41. It's probably impossible to find during the day in Sinai.
43. What one drinks out of (Heb.)
44. What the chance for peace sometimes seems to be.
45. The tragic classification of so many Israelis who fought in the Yom Kippur War (Eng. abbrev.)
47. Eligible Zionist Bachelors, Inc. (abbrev.)*
50. They got copper in this form from Solomon's mines.
51. Yosef Trumpeldor, heroic *chalutznik* killed in battle, said as he lay dying: *"It is good to ___ for our land."*
52. School teacher from Milwaukee, hero of the War of Liberation, Israel's 1st ambassador to the Soviet Union, 3rd Prime Minister of Israel.
58. The central figure in Israel's pre-statehood government, as well as the declarer of Israel's independence, and the State's 1st Prime Minister.
63. A printer's measure.
64. Europe's Jewish youth movements might be said to be the *"_____ mater"* of many *chalutzim.*
65. Bar _____ is one of Israel's major universities, and is largely religious.
66. Near East (abbrev.)

67. What the bush did when it wasn't consumed.
69. Who? (Heb.)
70. 1st word of many of the 10 Commandments (Heb.)

71. The Jewish calendar gives it 2 beginnings.
74. One of Israel's minorities, concentrated in the Golan.
76. In Israel, both children and plants grow in it.
77. United Nations Committee (abbrev.)*
79. Famous Israeli singer, _ _ _ _ _ Natan.
81. God took us out of Egypt with a *"strong hand and an outstretched _ _ _."*
82. It's half of every *aruchat arba.*
84. You're supposed to eat some just before fasting on Tisha B'Av.
86. Darwin said we all came from one; the Bible prefers to trace us to Adam.
87. Largest unit measure of Israeli currency.
89. Stereotype image of the rich, spoiled, Jewish female in the U.S. (abbrev.)
91. Israel's New Left Communist Party (Heb.)
93. Israel's largest agricultural export product.
94. The smallest measure of Israeli currency (plural).

95. First kibbutz, founded on the shores of #2 Across in 1910 by 9 men and 1 woman.
96. Israel's gone through too many of them already.
97. British document which gave the first modern, political, international legality to the future State of Israel, signed in 1917.

DOWN

1. The Jewish people have never ceased hoping, working, and praying for a time when life would be better, for the _ _ _ _ _ _ _ _ _ _ age.
2. What Arabs yell in the Old City for "watch out! "
3. Where the generation with a slave mentality died out, where we received the Torah, where the covenant was renewed; now the buffer zone between Israel and Egypt.
4. *"_ _ not _ _ unto others what you would not have them _ _ unto you"* — Hillel.
5. Exploration in this field constantly brings out new evidence of the ancient tie of the Jewish people to the Land of Israel.
7. A great prophet who preached the greater importance of righteous action than ritual sacrifice.
8. From the _ _ _ _ _ _ of _ _ _ _ _ _ _ you get a panorama view of the Old City of Jerusalem; on its slope is an ancient Jewish graveyard desecrated during Arab occupation of the city (1948-1967).
9. _ _ *vey!* Yiddish exclamation.
10. _ _ _ _ _ Sadat, president of Egypt after Nasser.
11. How your grandparents from Europe might have said "were" when they arrived in America.
12. It encompasses the meaning of Jewish peoplehood.

18. Maccabia is the name of Israel's team in the Olympic _ _ _ _ _ _. (Note: Due to the professional quality of this puzzle, the last two letters of this word are reversed. Sorry.)

19. The term applied to Jews of Spanish, African, or Arab-world descent; the group of Jews suffering the most social, educational, and economic hardship in Israel today.

20. Zionism, the _ _ _ _ _ _ _ _ liberation movement of the Jewish people.

21. Israel's near equivalent of M.I.T.

22. *"Next year in _ _ _ _ _ _ _ _ _ _;"* the 2000 year old focus of the Jewish people's dreams.

23. Egyptian Research and Educational Services for Doctors (abbrev.)*

28. Hebrew for "no" or "to him."

30. Egyptus Populous (abbrev.)*

36. *Medinat _ _ _ _ _ _ _*

38. Favorite spot for outings near the Dead Sea; also a hide-out for David in Biblical days.

40. English for the Hebrew *el* or *l'*.

42. French for the Hebrew *kacha, kacha* (כבה ככה) *comme _ _, comme ça.*

45. It's in the center of the Israeli flag; also, Israel's Red Cross: _ _ _ _ _ _ _ _ _ _ *Adom*

46. Many Jews can't get to Israel today because they live behind the _ _ _ _ curtain.

48. Mountain in Jerusalem from which came the name of the Jewish people's movement of national liberation.

49. Arye _ _ _ - _ _ _ _ _ _ _, active member of the Irgun in pre-statehood days, and Deputy Speaker of the Knesset in 1956. (Given in puzzle.)

53. The _ _ _ _ e are a national-religious minority in Israel, very loyal to the government and very active in the State's society.

54. He was created along with other animals on the sixth day of creation.

55. Hebrew for "to;" also, as in "_ _ Dorado cigars."

56. What Rachel is known as for every Jew (Heb.)

57. Israel's crops depend on it today as much as they did thousands of years ago; there's still a daily prayer for it during certain seasons.

58. Acrostic name of certain pioneers who came to Palestine from Russia beginning in 1882; taken from the Hebrew for the Biblical verse: *"O House of Jacob, Come ye and let us walk."* (Isaiah 2:5).

59. Amos _ _ _ _, famous Israeli author of the book: *The Israelis: Founders and Sons.*

60. Introductory Hebrew word indicating "please."

61. Where most of the Jews in America live: Greater New York (abbrev.)

62. Hebrew for "spirit" or "wind."

67. What people do all the time on Egged buses.

68. The Law of _ _ _ _ _ _ was Israel's first, providing automatic citizenship to any Jew who wishes it (with the exceptions of criminal and public health risks).

72. Levi _ _ _ _ _ _ was Israel's 2nd Prime Minister.

73. Singing after meals adds to the Shabbat _ _ _ c _ (Heb.)

75. There used to be a long one from Damascus to Cairo; you can see where it was cut off near Rosh Hanikra (abbrev.)

76. Para-military training that Israeli high school kids go through. (If you're lucky, you'll get to stay at one of their camps for a few days too!)

78. A fruit traditionally eaten on Tu B'Shvat.

80. The major socialist-oriented party in Israel, having received a plurality of votes in

every elections thus far (Eng. abbrev.)
83. Eastern Nomadic Association in Israel (abbrev.)*
85. Abraham's first wife.
88. Hebrew near equivalent to "far out!"
89. Each individual belonging to Israel's majority.
90. Some say the Yom Kippur War allowed the Arabs to feel militarily on ___ with the Israelis.
92. Association of Temple Fathers (abbrev.)*

* If such a group exists it's news to us, but put the abbreviations in place anyway; they hold the puzzle together.

A Thought

Those with Zionist beliefs are often accused of being particularists, in contradistinction to their repeated assertions of universalist convictions.

The accusers should perhaps recall their own childhood experiences of mixing together many different colors of fingerpaint. The inevitable result, you may recall, was a less than attractive color.

Perhaps what the world is in need of is a mosaic, and not a melting pot; an environment in which each people is given a land of its own; a situation of nations complementing each other, harmonizing, and held together by the grout of humanist concern.

Outside the land of Israel, to be a Jew is to have an identity.
Inside Israel where "Jew" is a common denominator, that is not enough.
One goes to Israel and realizes the emptiness of a label, but the fullness of humanity.

A Land Of Contrasts

Sometimes we don't think that Israel makes much sense. It's a country in which one sees apparent contradictions everywhere, and a place where a person can experience culture shock just by turning around. But what can one expect from a land which not only exudes so much ancient history, but which is also the home of a people struggling to create a vital, contemporary society?

Here's some room to keep a list of the contrasts you see which you feel are noteworthy, and to comment on them, of course, as you're so inspired.

New Jerusalem and ....

Egged buses and ....

Old Jews and ....

Tel Aviv and ....

Barren countryside and ....

Arab merchants and ....

Soldiers and ....

Keep the list going yourself:

Israel

A nation of contrasts. . . . a land of harmony . . .

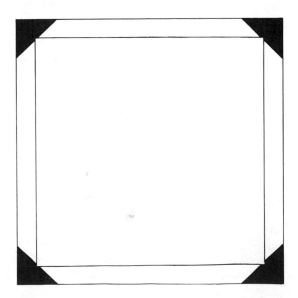

This page, and the others like it scattered throughout this book, are for your photographs. The descriptive phrases above are for your inspiration! Whatever other pictures you take, we suggest you try to get a few illustrating the ideas they express.

Word Dig

Look at this mess of letters and see how many words you can find (right to left, left to right, standing on your head, up and down, down and up, bumping on a bus, diagonally . . .). As you find a word, **circle** *it and* **think** *about it. What do you know about it? What don't you know about it? Do you know anything?*

```
A N M I D I S A H E S S U P O C S
T U R D A T S I H A D A S S A H F
A V O D A N A R E R E B P E R C A
T S V U H S I Y Z O A R A V U N T
E H U N E R A G U P O A L E I A E
X A L E B A N A R S H E M E N H S
T L J O R D A N D A W W A D I A S
I O A T E I F A R I E M C S G L E
L M F K W R A V A D I L H J E W N
E A F E M S I N O I Z T U B B I K
X A A D Y I D I O T M D D I N R A
I R G U N O A H R M A S S A D A R
L I O M R P D E T I N U A L U F A
E V D I A I H T-S A M A R I A K B
L E U M I S I M H A A L A K S A H
```

Note: All the letters can be used, but some of them only in transliterations of Hebrew words.

מה מיוחד?
Mah M'yuchad?

Here you are, finally in Israel. What was the first thing you can remember that made you feel it was for real?

Do you remember what you expected to find? Did you find it?

Are there certain things that keep coming up, reminding you where you are?

Something else. Those who live here, do they feel the same way you do? Is there anything special about Israel to them? Be brave and find out. Go up to all sorts of people on the street and ask: *"Mah m'yuchad b'Yisrael?"* (מה מיוחד בישראל) . It's one way to find out what it means, and we promise they won't hit you for saying it. (No guarantees about stares though.) Most will be glad to answer, but not necessarily in English. If you can't understand what they say, have them write down their responses here, and ask someone later on to translate for you. It's a great way to start talking to people, to begin to understand what makes them tick, and to find out what's important to those who have made Israel home. Do it. We assure you an experience.

An old religious Jew:

A teenager:

A soldier:

Anyone ....:

Anyone ....:

Anyone ....:

A Song

HATIKVA

התקוה

Kal od ba-ley-vav p'nimah
Nefesh Y'hudi homiyah
Ul'patai mizrakh kadimah
Ayin l'tzion tzofiah
Od lo avdah tikvateinu
Hatikvah mishnot alpayim
L'hiyot am khafshi b'artzenu
B'eretz tzion v'yerushalayim.

כל עוד בלבב פנימה
נפש יהודי הומיה.
ולפאתי מזרח קדימה
עין לציון צופיה.
עוד לא אבדה תקותנו
התקוה משנות אלפים,
להיות עם חפשי בארצנו,
בארץ ציון וירושלים.

So long as still within our breasts
The Jewish heart beats true,
So long as still towards the Easts,
To Zion, looks the Jew,
So long our hopes are not yet lost —
Two thousand years we cherished them —
To live in freedom in the land
Of Zion and Jerusalem.

Section 3
THE
ISRAEL CONNECTION

Now And Then

JEWISH HISTORY

GENERAL HISTORY

The Patriarchs — Abraham, Isaac, and Jacob — develop the earliest forms of monotheism and settle in *Eretz Yisrael*. Their descendants migrate to Egypt to escape famine and are eventually enslaved (2000—1500 BCE)

Egyptian dynasties
(Hyksos and others)
pyramids built

1500

After Exodus from Egypt (c. 1280 BCE), 40 years of wandering in the desert, and receiving the Torah, the people are rid of their slave mentality and prepared to return to *Eretz Yisrael* as an independent nation (1300—1050 BCE)

Egyptian Pharoah
Ramses
rules from
c. 1290—1224

1000

King David makes Jerusalem his capital (1000 BCE); his son King Solomon builds First Temple there; prophets urge social justice; kingdom divided into Judea and Israel (c. 930 BCE)

Mesopotamia and
Aram-Damascus
civilization flourish

Assyrians conquer Israel in 721 BCE; Babylonians conquer Judea in 586 BCE and destroy First Temple; Exile begins.

Sack of Thebes —
663 BCE

Return to *Eretz Yisrael* beginning 538 BCE and construction of 2nd Temple (mainly during 5th century BCE)

Fall of Nineveh in
Mesopotamia — 612 BCE

**500
BCE**

Hellenistic domination (323—168 BCE); Maccabean revolt restores Jewish autonomy 165 BCE

Alexander the Great
conquers Egypt (332 BCE)

**0
CE**

Roman domination intensifies and Jewish revolt begins 66 CE ending in failure with destruction of 2nd Temple 70 CE and conquest of Massada 73 CE; Exile

Assassination of Julius
Caesar in Rome — 44 CE

Bar Kochba leads last unsuccessful revolt against Romans (132—135 CE), after which Jewish population in *Eretz Yisrael* begins to decline until Jews become minority in 5th century CE

King Constantine rules —
306—337 CE

Mishna and Talmud appear, preserving constants in Jewish way of life regardless of place of residence (3rd—5th centuries)

End of Western Roman Empire — 476 CE

Jerusalem conquered by Arabs and Islamic rule begins — 638 CE

Justinian I — 527—565 CE

Jewish religion outlawed in Spain (694—711 CE)

Arabs conquer Spain — 711 CE

1000

First Crusades bring death and destruction to Jews along Rhine valley 1096

William of Normandy conquers England 1066

2nd Crusades 1146, Jewish communities in Germany and France massacred again

Anti-Jewish rioting throughout England with 3rd Crusade in 1189

Magna Carta 1215

Jews expelled from England in 1290

Jews expelled from France in 1306

100 Years War begins in 1337

Spanish Inquisition begins "reclaiming" Jewish souls by burning living bodies, 1480

Joan of Arc burned at the stake in 1431

Jews expelled from Spain in 1492 after centuries-long Golden Age of great prosperity and cultural advancement

Columbus discovers America 1492

1500

Jews expelled from Italy 1567

Luther publishes "95 Theses" in 1517

Shabbatai Zvi proclaims himself Messiah in 1665 and then betrays massive following by converting to Islam in 1666

Mayflower at Plymouth Rock 1620

Baal Shem Tov, founder of modern Hasidism, dies in 1760

Great London fire — 1666

Pale of Jewish Settlement established in Russia in 1791

American Revolutionary War 1776

Age of Enlightenment and Emancipation begins

Napoleon becomes Emperor 1804

Waves of immigration into Palestine begin in earnest with Biluim in 1882; migration

American Civil War 1861-5

almost exclusively from Europe and Russia

Herzl convenes 1st Zionist Congress in Basle in 1897

1900

Czar Alexander II assassinated 1881

Jewish rural settlement of Palestine begins with *chalutzim*; 1st kibbutz, Degania, established in 1909

Russo-Japanese War — 1904-5

Balfour Declaration — 1917, asserting England's recognition of right of Jews to national home in Palestine

1925

Russian Revolution; US enters World War I — 1917

6,000,000 Jews massacred in Nazi Holocaust during World War II (1939—1945)

Japan bombs Pearl Harbor — 1941

UN votes to partition Palestine (1947); Arabs reject plan and invade Jewish settlements in Palestine; War of Independence 1947-8

British colonial rule ends in India, 1947

David Ben-Gurion declares Israel's Independence — 1948

Korean War — 1950

1950

Sinai campaign — 1956

Six Day War — 1967; Jerusalem reunified

JFK assassinated, 1963

Russian Jews begin demonstrating in earnest for right to emigrate to Israel (1969)

Height of student unrest, 1968

War of Attrition — 1969-70

First man on the moon, 1969

Yom Kippur War — 1973

Israel agrees to territorial pullbacks from lands won in 1967 and 1973 wars — 1975

1975

Watergate Affair 1972-3

UN declares Zionism to be racism, 1975

David & Cindy, authors of this book, get married — 1975

Israel celebrates 28 years of Independence, 1976

US begins arms sales to Egypt, 1976; Patty Hearst found guilty

Israel commandos execute daring raid into Uganda, freeing Israeli hostages hijacked to Entebbe — 1976

2000 CE

Jimmy Carter elected president of U.S. — 1976

(Squeeze in events of your own life, to round out this list.)

Archaeology: Dead or Alive

Archaeology is practically a national pastime in Israel. Ask the people here what it means to them personally. Go ahead. Is it a matter of digging for roots? An effort to further legitimize their right to be here? A search for clues to their ancestors' way of life and the meaning life had for them? Are they seeking their own place in Jewish tradition and Jewish history? Or are they bored by the whole thing?

Seeing the ancient remains of synagogues, cities, and graveyards is a thing very dead to some, very alive to others. But at the very least, it is incontrovertible evidence that the Jewish people lived on this very spot thousands of years ago. Make of that what you will. And keep a record of your own feelings below.

Ancient sites I've been to — the ones I can remember:

PLACE	UNIQUE THING ABOUT IT, OBSERVATIONS, DETAILS, WHAT'S THERE TODAY, ETC.

PLACE	UNIQUE THING ABOUT IT ETC.

Every time I see an ancient ruin: *(check appropriate responses)*

( )   Joining a dig myself seems like an exciting possibility.
( )   I promise myself next time I'll stay on the bus.
( )   I feel a real link to all of Jewish history.
( )   I think it looks just like the last ruin I saw.
( )   I feel Israel really belongs to the Jews.
( )   I'm sure it looks just like the last ruin I saw.
( )   I can hardly comprehend what 2000 years means
( )   I'm amazed by how things uncovered compare to what we have today.
( )   I bet it *is* the last ruin I saw.

comment

Archaeology

Pictures of the Bible . . . foundations of today . . .

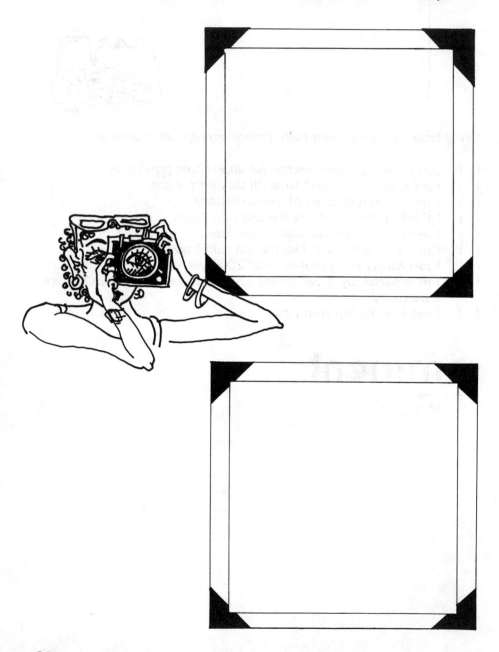

"Naturally" Jewish[2]

Centuries ago, the Jews were extremely involved with and concerned about the natural phenomena with which they lived. As farmers and shepherds they had to be; the better they knew the effects seasonal changes had on their crops, and the more they were acquainted with the life processes of their herds, the greater would be their productivity. Obviously without the kinds of scientific journals we have today to bring them the latest techniques in farming, they had to rely much more heavily on their own primary experience with nature.

One difference between them and other ancient peoples, was that the Hebrews connected all that went on around them to a single spiritual force. Thus the importance they placed on their surroundings became reflected in the rituals of their festivals; the wonders of nature became a basic theme in their psalms and prayers; and ways of protecting the world were made into their laws.

Although there was no Hebrew word for "ecology," these ancient Jews were probably more concerned with their environment than most of us are today. We don't mean to imply that Judaism is or ever was a nature religion, but it does seem to us that a good many Jewish ideas and ideals are rooted in Biblical concepts and understandings of nature, and that a substantial amount of Jewish life style evolved from the relationship and experiences with nature that the **People** of Israel had with the **Land** of Israel back during the time that the **Book** of Israel first came into being.

For those of you whom we've managed to stimulate enough to look into specifics, we've included just a few concrete examples of these ideas below.

IN THE HOLIDAYS

One example here to remember for next year's *Seder*: The bitter herb the *Haggada* tells us we eat to recall the bitterness of slavery has more of a story behind it than that. The Talmud tells us that during the *Seder* not only do we have to eat the bitter herb raw, but that that herb can only be chosen from among one of five specific types. These five, unlike any others known to the Rabbis, reportedly develop in pretty much the same way. Each year, when they first appear above ground, they're supposedly soft and rather good. As time goes on, they become a little tougher, and start losing their sweetness. They slowly become bitter, but for a while, if cooked, lose this bad taste. (It's around that point that we eat them on

Passover.) And finally, just after the *Pesach* season, they become absolutely inedible, even if boiled, dry up, and die. So what?

The Rabbis point out the parallel of this herb's development to the story of the Jews in *Eretz Mitzraim* (ארץ מצרים) . When our ancestors first arrived there, life was soft and sweet for them. As time went on, slavery made it tough and bitter, and then, just around the time we were taken out of Egypt, it was becoming unbearable. To us that's kind of neat: not only the parallel, but also that the Jews chose to remember the history of their lives in Egypt by making use of the nature they were now so dependent on, and which represented the whole new life they were now living.

This bitter herb which we eat, what does it mean? It is eaten because the Egyptians embittered ...

מרור זה שאנו אוכלים
על שום מה? על שום
שמררו המצריים.

"Why on this night **do** we eat *maror* (מרור) .. ?" Now you've got a fuller answer.

IN THE TEXTS

Most people read the following lines and just consider them to be beautiful love poetry and no more. You might not consider them to be even that. But read them anyway.

> Rise up my love, my fair one, and come away,
> For lo, the winter is past,
> The rain is over and gone;
> The [*nitzanim*] flowers appear on the earth;
> The time of singing [of the *zamir* bird] has come,
> And the voice of the turtle [turtledove] is heard in our land;
> The fig-tree putteth forth her green leaves,
> And the vines in blossom give forth their fragrance;
> Arise my love, my fair one, and come away;
> O my dove that art in the clefts of the rock, in the covert of the cliff,
> Let me see thy countenance, let me hear thy voice ...

— Songs of Songs, 2:10-14

To those who know the ecology of *Eretz Yisrael*, it is clear that these lines relate the cycle of nature within which the ancient Hebrews lived. Here: in Israel, the rainy season goes from October to March. By April the *nitzanim* (ניצנים) flowers begin to bud. A little later on the *zamir* (זמיר) bird which normally sings a monotonous tune, begins suddenly with a melodious mating call. Early in May the turtledove starts mating as well, and his voice, now also distinctive, can be heard all over the country. By the end of that month, the fig-trees and then the grapevines begin to ripen. And from May to June the doves too are beginning to pair off. Using the patterns of nature to get his message across, this poet is saying to his beloved that now it's their time . . .

If this kind of thing interests you enough, read Psalm 104 yourself and see what you can find in there about an appreciation for the balance of nature.

IN JEWISH LAW

As we've mentioned, the Jews also took care to preserve this nature. Notice how when the flood was coming, Noah was ordered to take at least two of every animal with him **male and female**, *"to keep them alive."* (Gen. 6:19-20) Two of the same sex just wouldn't have done the trick. Realize also how the ancient Hebrews were encouraged to plant for six years, but were commanded to let the fields lie fallow during the seventh, for *"the seventh year shall be a sabbath of solemn rest for the land."* (Leviticus 25:3-4) And note that even during battle the Jews were told to be careful of their surrounding: *"When thou shalt besiege a city . . . in making war against it . . . thou shalt not destroy the trees thereof . . . for is the tree of the field a man, that it would be destroyed by thee?"* (Deut. 20:19) And in regard to animals, it is forbidden to muzzle an ox while threshing grain (Deut. 25:24). This commandment has been

37

expanded into a decree that no undue physical temptation be placed before any worker — animal or person — if he or she be unable to attain it.

comment

Scramble

Unjumble the letters of each word below and write them correctly in the spaces provided.

D N A L Ⓞ Ⓞ _ _

E O P P E L _ _ _ _ _ Ⓞ

I L E B B _ Ⓞ _ _ _

I T I R S P Ⓞ _ _ Ⓞ _ _

Next, combine the circled letters of each of the component elements you've uncovered and put them together to find something that **is real**: _ _ _ _ _ _

(Answers appear on p.245.)

The Land, The People
And The Book

   With the way some Israelis give directions, we at times feel we'd be better off with an ancient map of the place from the Biblical period than to try to get information from a passer-by. True, it wouldn't help us get to Tel Aviv, but we'd certainly be able to find Jerusalem, Be'ersheva, Hevron . . .

   Anyway, here's a partial listing of places in Israel that are mentioned in the Bible. We've noted where; you take it from there. In other words, look them up.

ACCO — *Judges 1:31-32*

AFFULA (Biblical name: Ofel) — *II Kings 5:24*

ARAD — *Numbers 21:1; Joshua 12:14; Judges 1:16*

ASHKELON — *Zephania 2:7; II Samuel 1:20; Jeremiah 47:6; Amos 1:8*

BE'ERSHEVA — *Genesis 21:30,32; Genesis 26:32-33*

BEIT SHE'AN — *I Samuel 31:10*

BETHLEHEM — *Micah 5:1*

EILAT — *Deuteronomy 2:8; I Kings 9:26; II Chronicles 8:17*

EIN GEDI — *I Samuel 24:2; Song of Songs 1:14; Ezekiel 47:10*

GOLAN — *I Chronicles 6:56*

HAIFA (Mt. Carmel) — *I Kings 18:20-22, 36-38*

HEVRON (Kiryat Arba) — *Genesis 23:2; Genesis 23:19; II Samuel 5:1-3*

JAFFA — *Jonah 1:3*

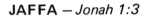

JERICHO — *Joshua 6:2-5*

JERUSALEM (Salem) — *Genesis 14:18; II Samuel 5:4-6; I Chronicles 11:14; I Kings 2:11*

JEZREEL VALLEY — *I Kings 21:1*

MEGGIDO — *I Kings 9:15*

MOUNT GILBOA — *II Samuel 1:19-27*

SEDOM — *Genesis 19:24*

comment Any feelings about actually being at places mentioned in the Bible? Try reading the verses about them while you're there.

The Land, The People

The connection . . .

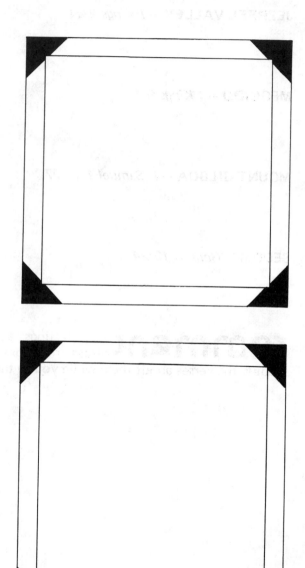

42

... And The Book

the interrelation . . .

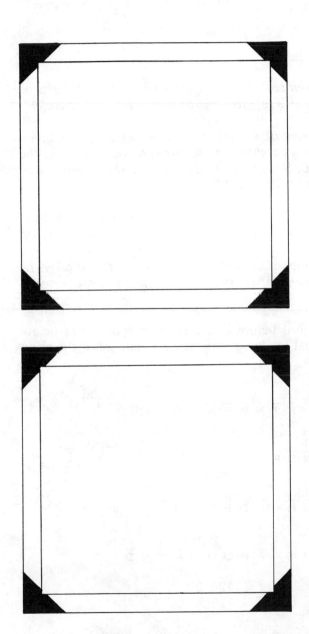

Crypto – Quotes

> Only in the soil that is Israel can the roots
> of the Jewish people be fully nourished.

The mass of letters printed below comprises intriguing tid-bits of Jewish philosophy on man's relationship to the world, and especially to nature.

Each given letter represents a different hidden letter. If the given letter is repeated, it always stands for the same hidden letter. In the example here, X=E, N=C, S=O, K=L, T=G, and L=Y. Fill them in and you should end up with "ECOLOGY."

$$\overline{X}\ \overline{N}\ \overline{S}\ \overline{K}\overline{S}\ \overline{T}\ \overline{L}$$ (hidden letters)

(given letters)

The code for each quotation is different, but hints are given to help you with each. Have fun! (If you have to give up, the answers appear on p.245.)

1. Hint: the fifth word below is the type of food we associate with Tu B'Shvat and that we hang from the Sukkah. Also, the given R = hidden O.

$$\overline{A}\ \overline{D}\ \overline{K}\ \overline{O} \quad \overline{N}\ \overline{D}\ \overline{R}\ \overline{X} \quad \overline{K}\ \overline{J}\ \overline{N}\ \overline{K}\ \overline{F}\ \overline{N} \quad \overline{N}\ \overline{D}\ \overline{K}$$

$$\overline{U}\ \overline{J}\ \overline{H}\ \overline{R}\ \overline{L} \quad \overline{R}\ \overline{T} \quad \overline{N}\ \overline{D}\ \overline{P} \quad \overline{D}\ \overline{J}\ \overline{O}\ \overline{S}\ \overline{F}'$$

$$\overline{D}\ \overline{J}\ \overline{W}\ \overline{W}\ \overline{P} \quad \overline{F}\ \overline{D}\ \overline{J}\ \overline{U}\ \overline{N} \quad \overline{N}\ \overline{D}\ \overline{R}\ \overline{X} \quad \overline{H}\ \overline{K}' \quad \overline{J}\ \overline{O}\ \overline{S}$$

$$\overline{Y}\ \overline{N} \quad \overline{F}\ \overline{D}\ \overline{J}\ \overline{U}\ \overline{U} \quad \overline{H}\ \overline{K} \quad \overline{A}\ \overline{K}\ \overline{U}\ \overline{U} \quad \overline{A}\ \overline{Y}\ \overline{N}\ \overline{D}$$

$$\overline{N}\ \overline{D}\ \overline{K}\ \overline{K}' \quad \text{--} \quad \overline{W}\ \overline{F}\ \overline{J}\ \overline{U}\ \overline{Q}\ \overline{F} \quad 128{:}2$$

2. Hint: Ever since Exile began, Jews have prayed for a
_ _ _ _ _ _ to Zion, the 4th word below.

A P T G   F R M   A Q S S   B T L M B G   L R

G J L M B T   F R M   A Q S S   D G R A   L P J L

F R M   P J C T   B T L M B G T N   L R   F R M B-

H T S O,   L P J L   A P T G   F R M   P Q N

O B R E   G J L M B T,   F R M   P Q N   O B R E

F R M B H T S O.   J. N.   I R B N R G

3. Hint: The 7th word below is at the end of your arm, and the
name of the pointer used for reading the Torah. 3rd word is a baby
tree.

B N   P   M P T O B F R   X S L S   B F   G D H L

Q P F U   P F U   G D H   X S L S   Y D O U   Y Q P Y

Y Q S   I S M M B P Q   Q P U   A D I S,

N B L M Y   T O P F Y   Y Q S   M P T O B F R,

Y Q S F   R D   P F U   R L S S Y   Q B I.

L P K K B   G D W Q P F P F   K S F   J P V P B

4. Hint: The 7th word below is what it takes to make forests. Also, H=A, R=N M=F, and P=U.

H̄   B H R'Ā   O C̄ M̄ K   C̄ Ā   Ā P Ā G H C R K J

L̄ N̄   G V̄ K K Ā.   Q̄ P Ā G   H Ā   T̄ G S K V Ā

S̄ H D̄ K   Y O H R G K J   M T V̄   N T P̄,   Y O H R G

M T V̄   Ḡ S K   Ā H E K   T M̄   N T P V

X̄ S C O J V K R.   ⁻ N H O E P G   Ā S C B T R C

5. Hint: Last 4-letter word is repeated twice in the first line of the *sh'ma* in English. 6th word is the large expanse of land we grow things on.

R̄ P F   N̄ O S̄   N̄ E S S   J̄ M   N̄ O S̄   M̄ Q S G F

B O R̄ G G   Z Q S G F   Q̄ N B   M E C Q̄ N   R P F

N̄ O S̄   S̄ R E N̄ O   B O R G G   Z Q S G F   Ō S E

Ā E J F C D S   R P F   N̄ O S Z   B O R G G   H S

B̄ R M S   Q̄ P   N̄ O S Q E   G R P F   R P F

N̄ O S Z   B O R G G   L P J X   N̄ O R N̄   Q   R Ū

N̄ O S   G J E F.   ⁻⁻ S̄ K S L Q S G   34:27

46

קיבוץ
Kibbutz

WARNINGS TO BE HEEDED UPON ENTERING A KIBBUTZ

1. Israel is not one big kibbutz, contrary to popular opinion held abroad. It is not even a small one. There are only two places where you'll hear that it is: one is at fund-raising dinners where they try to project an ideal image of the Jewish State, and the other is on any kibbutz you visit. Actually only some 100,000 Israelis are kibbutz-niks, but as they founded their way of life to be a model for a new society, they have a hard time adjusting to the fact that their 230 settlements comprise only some 3-3½% of the Israeli population.

2. Israel is one big kibbutz. You might have read elsewhere that it isn't, but let that be a lesson that you can't believe everything you read. The number of kibbutzniks influential in government, in the army, in the labor movement, and in other of Israel's institutions makes the effect of kibbutz life on Israeli society immeasurable. That doesn't mean everyone here picks oranges wearing one of those funny little hats, but it does mean the socialist ethic, intimacy in relationships, and gossip are widespread.

In order to find out what kibbutz life is really all about, you have to live on one for a good long time. Since you probably don't have a good long time at the moment, the best you can hope for is a good short time. In the visit you make to kibbutz try to discover as many bits and pieces as you can about the ideology, about the day to day life, and about the "institutions" that give the agricultural commune its uniqueness and flavor.

When talking to people on kibbutz, you might try to bring the conversation around to some of the ideas expressed below (which are quotations from Muki Tsur's booklet listed under "Reading into it . . .").

1. *"For the dreamers, it is an attempt to create a new society. For the cynics it is one of many attempts to change man, and will inevitably fail."*

2. *"Based on the idea of absolute freedom, the new society these groups dreamt about would be one without laws or limitations."*

3. *"To develop any understanding of the Israeli kibbutz today, one should probably start with the first fact of kibbutz life, the concept of equality."*

4. *"In socialist and Zionist circles, labor was held to be the most revolutionary activity."*

5. *"Originally, general assemblies of the kibbutz served as the prototype of today's encounter group."*

6. *"The Jewish daughter no longer identified herself with her mother the homemaker, but with the woman who chose prison, was exiled, or was condemned to death in her struggle against oppression."*

7. *"The repression of art was a self-imposed trend begun by the founders of the kibbutz."*

8. *"In the commune of today, as in the original kibbutzim, the members are students and intellectuals who identify with the oppressed and working people."*

Experience for yourself, or ask kibbutzniks about experiencing:

1. the behavior in the kitchen . . .

2. knowing everything about everyone . . .

3. not being woken up at night by babies . . . or going back to having kids sleep in the parents' houses . . .

4. having to sign up in advance to use a car . . .

5. hiring outside laborers . . .

6. doing manual labor for so many years . . .

7. being the boss in the kibbutz factory . . .

8. seeing that the women are the ones taking care of the kitchen, laundry, and the children . . .

9. eating with 300 people every night . . .

10. not really owning anything . . .

11. having to get the community's permission to go on to advanced studies or to travel abroad . . .

12. participating in general assembly meetings . . .

13. children of the kibbutz leaving the settlement . . .

14. the *hora* . . .

Try to find out what the following are all about:

1. *beit yeladim* (בית ילדים)

2. *chadar haochel* (חדר האוכל)

3. *sadran avodah* (סדרן עבודה)

4. *machsan begadim* (מכסן בגדים)

5. *aruchat arba* (ארוחת.ארבע)

6. *mo'adon* (מועדון)

7. *meshek* (משק)

8. *chaver* (חבר)

9. *v'adot* (ועדות)

10. *aseyfa clalit* (אסיפה כללית)

Also, while we're on communal settlements, find out what you can about two more types: *moshav ovdim* (מושב עובדים) and *moshav shitufi* (מושב שיטופי) The latter is especially important, as we live on one!

comment And put it all together:

Living Off The Land

Somehow, though you may hate mowing the lawn at home, picking apples on a kibbutz just might not be that bad. And though the labor fifty years ago was much harder than it is today, the early pioneers (חלוצים) , many of them from comfortable, bourgeois homes, voluntarily — and eagerly — came to a countryside neglected for thousands of years. Though the environment was generally less than hospitable, they joined together in the task of watering the desert in the south, drying up the swamps in the north, and cultivating the hills and valleys inbetween.

There was a principle the *chalutzim* were operating by known as *kibbush avodah* (כיבוש עבודה) , or "the conquest of labor," and the idea behind it was that the Jews themselves had to start doing all the jobs necessary to run a country. As long as one contributed what he or she could, then it didn't matter whether an individual was a street cleaner or a doctor. In fact, there was no greater contribution one could make to the Jewish revolution than to become a manual laborer. Everyone was to feel they were helping to build the country.

> Splendid is the study of Torah
> when combined with a worldly occupation.
> Study which is not combined with work
> becomes the cause of sin
>
> Pirke Avot.

comment Here's a place to discuss with yourself any experience you might have of direct contact with the Land: planting a tree, working on a kibbutz or *moshav,* falling off a camel, or whatever. It's also a place where you might comment on the general attitude towards labor you sense around you, or on specific phenomena such as Arabs comprising some 90% of the construction workers here today.

The Land

Living . . . and lived on . . .

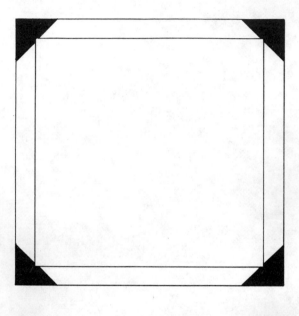

STRUGGLE
AND RESISTANCE

Section 4

תשעה באב
Tisha B'Av

Besides Shabbat, *Tisha b'Av* (תשעה באב) is the only day of the Jewish calendar we mention in this book. The reason for this is that, as a summer event, it's one that Jewish organizations, synagogues, and schools often don't get around to commemorating. If you're in Israel for the summer you'll certainly be aware of it, and wherever you are, you should deal with its significance.

Tisha b'Av — the 9th day of the month of Av — is a day of mourning and remembering, a day to really try to understand the suffering of the Jewish people, endured throughout our long and often tragic history. Many disasters have befallen the Jewish people on and around this same day in different generations, but it evolved as and continues to be devoted primarily to the commemoration of the destruction of the First Temple in 586 BCE and the Second Temple in 70 CE which both occurred at this time. The sadness of the day, however, is evoked not only by the commemoration of the events themselves, but by their consequences as well: *the exile of the Jews from Jerusalem and Eretz Yisrael and the beginning of the Diaspora; i.e. the separation of our people from our Land.*

The culture, the prayers, the folklore, and the life style of the Jewish people — all having emerged from the involvement of the ancient Hebrews with the Land of Israel — were somewhat out of place in the countries of Exile (גלות). But still, the Jews, at least enough of them to keep things going, refused to give all that up, and for almost 2000 years continued to live and celebrate all that had been familiar to them in Israel. Jerusalem remained the focus of their thoughts, and *Tisha b'Av* naturally became their greatest day of mourning.

Beginning with the 17th of Tammuz, the day on which the city walls were first breached, the three weeks before *Tisha b'Av* are solemn ones. And starting with the first of Av, religious custom prohibits eating meat, drinking wine, going to entertainment, and so on, all customary Jewish signs of mourning. Then, the eve of *Tisha b'Av* itself marks the beginning of a fast that ends at sundown the next day. *Eicha* (איכה), the book of Lamentations (which deals with the destruction of Jerusalem) is read. Kinot (כינות – a collection of reflections on tragedy and hope) are studied, and those portions of the Talmud which deal with the destruction of the Temples are learned.

People sit on the floor chanting and learning these crucial moments of our history by candlelight. Try getting some people together to read something of all this; the day is an important one.*

In addition to this studying, leather, jewelry, and perfume are not worn; washing is prohibited; sleeping without a pillow and sitting on the floor instead of on chairs are customary; and marital relations are forbidden. By being just a little uncomfortable ourselves, we're in a better position to think about and come to terms with the meaning of the day.

In 1967, with the *Kotel* (כותל), the Western Wall, liberated from Arab occupation, some people broke their fast after half a day (or didn't fast at all) and rejoiced. But most have continued to look at the Wall not content only to exclaim how wonderful it was that we have it back. They remember that what they are seeing is only a retaining wall of the Temple courtyard, and really isn't very much to have retrieved at all. They look at it and see ruins, and think how pitiful it is that this pile of stones is all that is left of the vibrant, thriving society that lived here 2000 years ago. And they are inspired

* You might also want to get hold of *Readings for Tisha B'Av*, an excellent collection of material from varied sources. It's available from Youth and Hechalutz (address in "Looking for something?").

to rebuild Israel today, to recapture the valuable aspects of the past, and to once again live in a society fully involved with its land. They remember how many people we have lost — so many so recently — and *Tisha b'Av* becomes not only a day of mourning, but also a day of conviction to the Zionist ideal of peacefully restoring a people to its land.

We believe that the Jewish spirit demands of us such an attitude, for our tradition claims that on this very day the Messiah will be born. Mourning, yes. Meditation, yes. But no sense of desperation, or resignation to suffering. We must certainly remember the bitterness of exile — to the extent of feeling personally that in our past we ourselves were once conquered — but we are not to become enslaved now to the desire for vengeance, as we were once enslaved to our conquerors. Should the long awaited birth take place **this** ninth day of the month of Av, each of us has the task of assuring the Messiah that it is not revenge, but redemption, that we seek. We dare not deny the past, but neither dare we deny the future.

Still, the day has a different personal meaning for everyone.

Putting Things In Perspective

We need but scan any time-line of our history to come away with the feeling that as long as we will maintain the Jewish tradition, so the world will maintain its own. Jewish history indeed appears vicious, and at times without solace. Explaining the tragedies that have befallen us goes beyond any political or social theory. But we must also realize that our view of history is a limited one. At the risk of oversimplifying — and certainly with no intention of making light of our suffering — we nevertheless contend that there may be a meaning to it all beyond our immediate comprehension.

Contemplate the dots below. View each as an isolated event of our history, and there seems to be no connection between them at all.

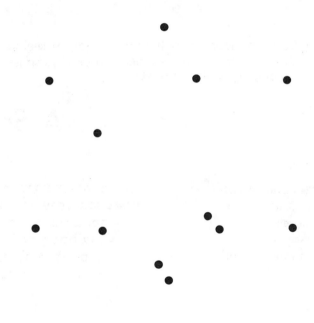

But seen from a slightly different perspective . . .

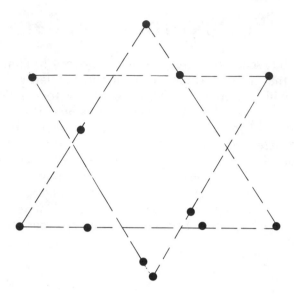

Maybe along with the Messiah will come a way of seeing things that will ease the pain of what has been, and a promise for a harmony that will encompass all of humankind.

A Song

ANI MA'AMIN

אני מאמין

Ani ma'amin b'emunah shlemah
B'viat hamashiach, ani ma'amin,
V'af al pi sh'yitmameyha
Im kal zeh akhakeh lo;
Akhakeh lo b'kel yom sh'yavo,
Im kal zeh ani ma'amin.

אני מאמין באמונה שלמה
בביאת המשיח, אני מאמין,
ואף על פי שיתמהמה –
עם כל זה אחכה לו;
אחכה לו בכל יום שיבוא,
עם כל זה אני מאמין.

I believe with complete faith
In the coming of the messiah, I believe,
And even though he delays —
With all that I will wait for him;
Every day I will wait for him to come,
With all this I believe
   —Jewish folk tune

הכותל
The Wall

think To many it is simply a useless collection of stones, a meaningless reminder of a time long gone. To others it is a heartbreaking pile of ruins, all that is left of a full Jewish culture that must now be restored. Legends tell of a cooing dove, perched 'til this very day on the Wall, lamenting the destruction of this glory.

read When I saw the Wall for the first time, I felt:

( ) mystical   ( ) Jewish
( ) tiny   ( ) overwhelmed
( ) out of place   ( ) nothing
( ) spiritual   ( ) surprised at myself
( ) disappointed   ( ) _____

        ( ) all of the above
        ( ) still trying to figure it out

       (X) Let me explain:

There's so much to say: about what people had told me I'd feel, and about what I actually felt; about the people who were there, and about me being among them; about what 2000 years means, and about *"Next year in Jerusalem"* . . .

ALSO Walk to the *Kotel* (everyone can tell you where it is) late at night with some friends. Look at the Wall as it stands in the moonlight, ignoring the floodlights if you can. Compare the scene with the way it appears on Shabbat, on *Tisha b'Av,* or on any old day. Find a picture, or someone's recollection, of what the area looked like in 1947.

connect *"The entire nation was exalted and many wept when they heard of the capture of the Old City. Our Sabra youth, and most certainly our soldiers, do not tend to be sentimental, and they shrink from any public show of feeling. But the strain of battle, the anxiety which preceded it, and the sense of salvation and of direct confrontation with Jewish history itself cracked the shell of hardness and shyness and released wellsprings of emotion and stirrings of the spirit. The paratroopers who conquered the Western Wall leaned on its stones and wept — in its symbolism an act so rare as to be almost unparalleled in human history. Rhetorical phrases and clichés are not common in our Army, but this scene on the Temple Mount, beyond the power of words to describe, revealed as though by a flash of lightning truths that were deeply hidden."*

— Yitzhak Rabin

know The Western Wall (also known as the "Wailing Wall," or *Hakotel Hamaravi* in Hebrew) was only the western support of the Temple Mount, and is actually the third wall out from the Temple itself. Still, it is the only part of the Temple area remaining in existence after the destruction of the Second Temple by the Romans in 70 CE, and therefore of great importance to both the religious and national consciousness of the Jewish people.

Around 1520, the Wall became a permanent feature in Jewish tradition as the Turkish Sultan Selim conquered Jerusalem, uncovered it, and permitted the Jews to pray there. In December 1947, Arab attacks prevented Jews from approaching the Wall, and after May 1948, when the Jewish Quarter was occupied by the Arabs, Jews were unable to even see it. It was finally liberated on the third day of the Six Day War (June 7, 1967) by the parachutists of the Israel Defense Forces.

At present the area is being excavated and developed. To date, digging has uncovered a surface of the Wall as far down below the ground as the height that can be seen above ground! What is seen today consists of some seven layers of huge Herodian stone from the Second Temple period, four layers of plainer stone from Roman or Byzantine times, a number of yards of Arab or Mamaluk construction from the 7th century, and then several feet of smaller stones added within the past century to prevent objects from being thrown from the far side of the Wall onto the Jews praying below.

The Wall

Stones . . . and visions . . .

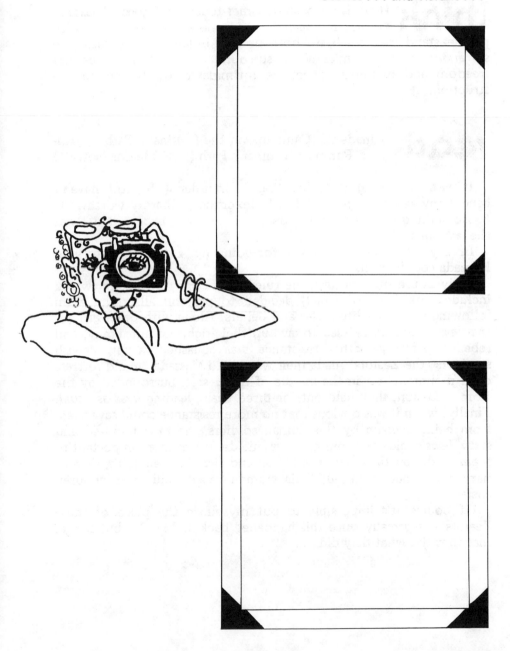

מצדה
Massada

think There is a slogan in Israel today that goes: *"Massada will not fall again!"* Once more in history the Jewish people stand as a small stubborn nation, isolated, but refusing to surrender to the enemies which surround it. The Jewish ideals of freedom and morality cannot be intimidated by threats of destruction.

read I made it! Came up via the ( )Snake Path ( )Roman Ramp ( )Runner's Path ( )Cable Car (softy!)

It was: ( )tiring ( )exhausting ( )murder ( )I still haven't caught my breath ( )lots of fun ( )exciting ( )hardly worthwhile ( )something I'm glad I did — once! ( )great — except that I was the last one up! ( ) _____

In any case, there's a reason for going up. Briefly the story of Massada goes like this:

Early in the first century, the rulers of the Roman Empire (which included the Land of Israel) decided to prohibit all groups from following their own life styles and beliefs. Along with other groups, the Jewish people refused to give up their rights of autonomy, and rebelled. After all other resistance was squashed, a few Jewish survivors (the Zealots) made their way up to Massada, an old fortress on a mountain top in the middle of the desert. Surrounded by the Roman Legion, they held out for three years, leading *lives as usual*. Finally, when it was obvious that no more resistance could save them from being overrun by the Roman soldiers, the nine hundred and sixty Jews decided to commit mass suicide. It was more important to them to die by their own hand, free and firm in their faith, than to have their men tortured, their women raped, and their children enslaved.

Of course it's impossible to put myself in the place of these Zealots — especially since this happened back in 73 CE — but to me, that they did what they did . . .

Also, there's something referred to here as the "Massada complex." It's the idea that life in Israel today reflects a similar attitude of living under a state of siege. How much is this the case? Well, from what I can make of the people living here . . .

connect *"My loyal followers, long ago we resolved to serve neither the Romans nor anyone else but only God; . . . now the time has come that bids us prove our determination by our deeds . . .*

"After all we were born to die . . . But outrage, slavery, and the sight of our wives led away to shame with our children — these are not evils to which man is subject by the laws of nature: men undergo them through their own cowardice if they have a chance to forestall them by death and will not take it . . .

"Pity the young whose bodies are strong enough to survive the prolonged torture; pity the not-so-young whose old frames would break under such ill usage. A man will see his wife violently carried off; he will hear the voice of his child crying 'Daddy!' when his own hands are fettered. Come! while our hands are free and can hold a sword, let them do a noble service! Let us die unenslaved by our enemies, and leave this world as free men in company with our wives and children."

Following this inspiration offered by the Zealots' leader, Eleazar Ben-Yair, Josephus Flavius records what took place:

> "And when ten of them had been chosen by lot to be the executioners of the rest, every man lay down beside his wife and children . . ., flung his arms around them, and exposed his

throat to those who must perform the painful office. These unflinchingly slaughtered them all, then agreed on the same rule for each other, so that the one who drew the lot should kill the nine and last of all himself."

know

Massada is located at the top of an isolated mountain plateau on the edge of the Judean desert and Dead Sea valley. Originally built by King Herod as a royal fortress for himself, it was eventually to become instead the last outpost of Jewish resistance during the same war in which the Second Temple and Jerusalem were destroyed (66-73 CE).

The story of the Zealots' last hours atop the mountain was related to Josephus Flavius (Jew turned Roman historian) by two women and their children who chose not to participate in the mass suicide. Josephus records that when the Romans finally penetrated the fortress they found evidence that the Jews had had enough food and water to last them for years, and recent archaeological expeditions (conducted by Yigael Yadin between 1963-65) indicate that the Jews were indeed living a "normal" life under siege: a *mikveh* (מקוה – ritual bath), synagogue, Biblical texts, and numerous coins are only a few of the hundreds of finds testifying to the fact.

The first modern spotting of Massada was made in the mid-19th century, and today, many excavations and thousands of tourists later, the recruits of Israel's Armored Corps swear their oath of allegiance on its summit.

Massada

Ideologues . . . and heroes . . .

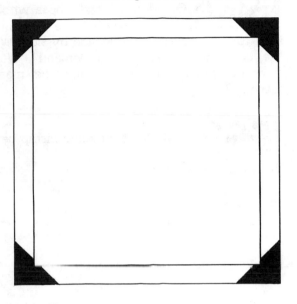

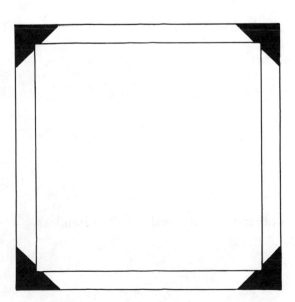

Mt. Herzl

think On Mount Herzl, those who laid down the ideology for the Jewish State and those who laid down their lives for the Jewish State lie side by side. Were the former aware of the cost their ideals would demand? Were those who paid the awesome price able to envision the meaning of their ultimate sacrifice?

read What about the relationship between:

Basle and Jerusalem?

Herzl's vision and today's Israel?

ideologues and soldiers?

casualties and victories?

you and Mount Herzl and all it implies?

connect It wasn't until he was 35 years old that Herzl became actively concerned with the "Jewish problem." But from the moment he did, his commitment was absolute. So, apparently, was his appreciation for the great implications of the task he was undertaking. In the first entry of his diaries, dated Shavuot, 1895, he wrote:

> "For some time past I have been occupied with a work of infinite grandeur. At the moment I do not know whether I shall carry it through. It looks like a mighty dream. But for days and weeks it has possessed me beyond the limits of consciousness; it accompanies me wherever I go . . .
>
> "It is still too early to surmise what will come of it, but my experience tells me that . . . it is something remarkable and that I ought to write it down."

What did come of it was **The Jewish State**, a book published in 1896 which so excited people about the possibility of return and self-determination that he was encouraged to the point of convening the First Zionist Congress in Basle in 1897. That he placed great hope in the conference can be inferred from his opening remarks to the assembled delegates:

> "There is much to be accomplished within the space of three days. We want to lay the foundations of the edifice which is one day to house the Jewish people . . . On this solemn occasion . . . Jews have come together from so many lands . . . Should we not be stirred by a premonition of great events when we remember that at this moment the hopes of thousands upon thousands of our people depend on our assemblage? . . . Enlightenment and comfort should go forth from this Congress. Let everyone find out what Zionism really is . . . a moral, lawful, humanitarian movement, directed toward the long-yearned-for goal of our people."

Prophetically aware from the beginning of the dimensions of what he was doing, Herzl wrote of the Congress in his diary on September 3, 1897:

"If I were to sum up the Basle Congress in a word — which I shall guard against doing publicly — it would be this: At Basle I founded the Jewish State.
"If I said this out loud today, I would be met by universal laughter. Perhaps in five years, and certainly in fifty, everyone will know it . . ."

On November 29, 1947 — exactly fifty years later — the United Nations voted the establishment of a Jewish State. But Herzl, had he still been alive, would himself not have been content to rest with that. In an address to young people in 1904 he said:

"And I sincerely believe that even after our country, Eretz Yisrael, will be ours, the vision of the Zionist movement will not dissolve. For Zionism, according to my perspective, is not an endeavor limited to the securing of a legally recognized land for our unfortunate people, but that there is also in it striving and struggle for moral and spiritual integrity."

know Mount (*Har* – הר) Herzl was named as such when Theodor Herzl's remains were reinterred there in 1949. The hill holds a museum built in honor of the man, a national cemetery in which many of the leaders and prophets of the Jewish State have been buried, and a military cemetery in which thousands of Israel's young and old war dead have been laid to rest.

Theodor (Binyamin Ze'ev) Herzl himself was born in Budapest in 1860. Though known as the father of modern Zionism, he was at first a prominent European lawyer and journalist who had almost completely abandoned his Jewish heritage. A number of events, climaxing with his coverage of the Dreyfus Affair (an anti-Semitic French trial) in 1895, led him to his conclusion that political Zionism, culminating in the establishment of an autonomous Jewish entity, was the only viable answer to the "Jewish problem." He was responsible for gathering the first Zionist Congress in Basle in 1897, and although he died at the early age of 44 (in 1904), only eight years after his commitment to Zionism became firm, his vision has guided Israel's founders and leaders in much of their thinking right through to our time.

Mt. Herzl

From Holocaust . . . to Statehood . . .

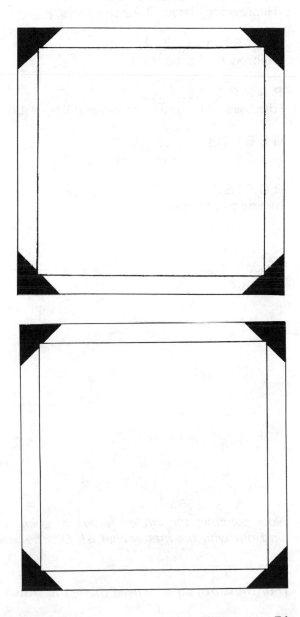

Scramble

Here are some of the ingredients for one recipe for the State of Israel. Unjumble the letters of each word below and write them correctly in the spaces provided.

H L A Z A T _◯_◯_◯
(Hebrew for "Israel Defence Forces")

B A T S H A B ◯◯_ _ _ _◯
(Hebrew for "Sabbath")

R A H O T _◯◯_ _
(the basis of all of Jewish law and life, Hebrew)

G E E V N _◯_◯_
(it's dry, brown, and barren)

R O P I S A A D ◯_ _ _ _◯◯_
(where all the Jews not in Israel are)

Now combine the circled letters of each word you've formed, and find out who the master chef is! Or: the Jewish George Washington.

_ _ _ _ _ _ _ _ _ _ _ _

(For those of you who need them, the answers appear on page 245.)

תל חי
Tel Hai

think The last words of Yosef Trumpeldor, defender of Tel Hai, were: *"It is good to die for our country."* (טוב למות בעד ארצנו) . It is also good to have a country in which to believe so deeply. Without the vision and commitment of such people as these early pioneers, a Jewish State would most certainly not have come into being in 1948.

read Give some thought to just how far you're willing to go in standing up for what you believe in ... to martyrdom ... to the sacrifice Zionism has demanded of the Jewish people ... to the memory of Israel's heroes ... to the meaning of a Jewish State ... to heroism, nationalism, and patriotism both here and where you come from ...

connect Following World War I, the region of the Upper Galilee was officially divided between French and English occupation, and simultaneously settled by Arab and Jewish nationalists. The friction between the parties involved was intense, and Tel Hai was one of three outposts thus established to look out for Zionist interests. Excerpts from Trumpeldor's diaries and letters give us a glimpse into the lives and thoughts of the community's inhabitants:

January 4, 1920:

"The question, whether it was expedient to flee ... hovered in the air, but no one at Tel Hai dared give it utterance. On the contrary, at the meeting that was hastily convened, it was definitely resolved to remain where we were at all costs ... When the decisive moment came, we would fight for our existence to the utmost limit, and we would, of course, try and sell our lives as dearly as possible ..."

January 5, 1920:

' "... We have not enough men ... and not all of them are armed with rifles ... We need 1,000 ... rounds per rifle, but we have only 100. We have no hand grenades at all, nor have we machine guns. Our food stocks are becoming depleted. Even our stock of flour is low, so that in another week we shall actually face starvation ..."

January 6, 1920:

"... the situation continues to be grave ... but we were in good spirits, and we sang and joked. Even the girls ... did not falter for a moment ..."

January 12, 1920:

"... We are carrying on with the work in the fields under a group of guards. We are making haste to utilise the precious days to sow wheat ..."

February 9, 1920:

"... The hour of trial has almost come. It may happen tomorrow in all its horror ...

"... A new generation, a generation of sons of Eretz Yisrael, of free men, are standing on the frontier, ready to sacrifice their lives in order to hold it ..."

Undated, after February 21, 1920:

"... More men are badly needed ... You must send us at least twenty men, by Friday at the latest. Why have no women come?"

A few days later, Trumpeldor suffered his fatal wounds. It was as he was being evacuated to Kfar Giladee, a neighboring settlement, that he uttered his famous last words, and died.

know Tel Hai (Hill of Life) was established in 1918 by *Hashomer*, an association for Jewish self-defense. The settlement's purpose was to guard over Jewish land in northern Palestine.

Spurred on in part by French plans for the area, Arab nationalists attacked Tel Hai in 1920. Its heroic defense served at the time as a

great inspiration to all of the *Yishuv* (ישוב — Jewish community in Palestine), and has since become a symbol in Israel of the purest form of Jewish patriotism.

A massive roaring Lion of Judah today marks the graves of Yosef Trumpeldor and the seven young men and women who fell alongside him. And a museum there stands as monument to the daily struggles of this early community's pioneer settlers, and to the battle in which some were killed.

A cemetery for others who struggled in defense of the *Yishuv* also exists at the site, as does a youth hostel which hosts, among others, members of Israeli youth movements on their annual commemorative pilgrimages to the scene of the battle.

Yosef Trumpeldor himself was born in Russia in 1880. He was throughout his life noted for bravery in battle, first in the Russo-Japanese War, and later in the Zion Mule Corps, which he created with the authority of the British as an auxiliary unit during World War I. His specific contribution to the Zionist cause was his vision of, and active involvement in, establishing agricultural communes in *Eretz Yisrael* capable of fending for themselves. His mission began with organizing Zionist youth in Russia, England, and Palestine (he was leader of the widespread *Hechalutz* — The Pioneer — movement), and led eventually to his untimely death on Adar 11, 5680 (March 1, 1920) at Tel Hai, from where he was coordinating the defense of all settlements in the Upper Galilee.

Tel Hai

A settlement . . . and a memorial . . .

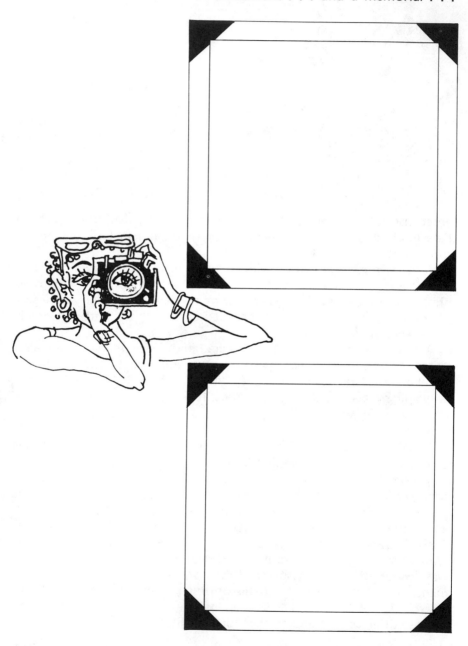

יד ושם
Yad Vashem

think It seems almost impossible to build a memorial to something that the mind can't even comprehend. And to research and document such horrors seems almost sacrilegious. Yet Yad Vashem (Monument and Memorial) exists as a major institution in Israeli life. No one grows up without visiting it, and many, many are related to those whom it commemorates.

react As difficult as it might be, try to put down some of your personal feelings about the place and what it stands for.

connect After each gassing of several hundred Jews in one of the "showers," the *sonderkommand*, a Jewish work detail, was forced to drag the corpses out to the crematoria, always faced with the possibility of recognizing a relative among the almost unrecognizable bodies. On one horrible occasion an even worse discovery was made: the *sonderkommand* came across the body of a young, emaciated girl; her eyes, full of horror, were still alive, her naked body was still giving out a slight pulse. Apparently she had ended up in a position which allowed her mouth to be in a corner with some moisture, somehow partially neutralizing the effect of the gassing. Immediately the *sonderkommand* brought her to a Jewish doctor in the camp whom the Germans had "recruited." He struggled endlessly, and finally brought her back to full consciousness. To his knowledge, she was the only victim of the gassing ever to be removed from the chamber alive. And now she had even regained her senses. Although she was but a single life saved among millions dead, the Jewish doctor and *sonderkommand* felt a complete victory in the saving of her life.

Just hours after her recovery was made known, a member of the German S.S. came and put a bullet through her head.[3]

know *Yad Vashem* on *Har Hazikaron* (Memorial Mountain) in Jerusalem is Israel's national monument to those who died and suffered in the Nazi Holocaust. As such, it serves: 1) to gather information on and perpetuate the memory of those individuals, communities, organizations, and institutions destroyed by the Germans, 2) to research and document individual and organized resistance to the Nazi regime, and 3) to spread the messages of the Holocaust by publishing a wide assortment of writings on the subject. Included on the site are a Memorial Hall (*Ohel Yizkor*), a synagogue, a museum, a garden of the Righteous Gentiles (with trees planted in appreciation and honor of those non-Jews who helped save Jews during the War), and the Hall of Names containing a still incomplete list of the victims.

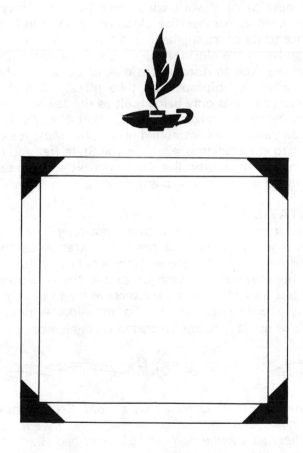

Challenge Of Faith

The Holocaust is not an easy subject with which to deal. We do not know how to invoke the memory of the Six Million in a manner befitting their deaths. Are we to live because they died? Or would they prefer to be left alone? But then, to whom do we owe allegiance, and to what avail? Perhaps our efforts should today be directed at developing a world-wide sense of community. But does anyone else even remember the Holocaust? Or care? Should we instead concentrate on strengthening the Jewish people? Or should our devotion be to the glorification of the individual? Or of God? Yet how are we even to discover the meaning of a God that exists in a world in which a Holocaust can take place? And then there is Israel: a nation that was only being built as the Jewish community in Europe was being terrorized, a nation that literally lives with a concentration camp number tatooed on its arm. Must it exist so as to bear witness to the catastrophe? Or is the State free and unfettered, belonging only to those who live there, permitted to create a life of its own, founded on any past and any premise it so desires?

CONFRONTATION...

One who struggles constantly with the meaning of the Holocaust is Elie Wiesel, once an inmate of the concentration camps, today a "messenger from the dead." His writings leave us confused. But that, perhaps, is his purpose: to teach us to ask the questions that will clarify and put into context the answers we try to live by. He relates to humanity. To feeling. To life. To meaning. And to God. The following three quotations are excerpted from his work:

Years after the war I learned that an old Rebbe from my little town in Hungary was now living in New York. I went to visit him, and found that he looked exactly as he always had . . .

"Has nothing changed?" I asked him.

"Nothing."

"What about me?"

"You haven't changed either."

"And Auschwitz? What do you make of Auschwitz?"

"Auschwitz proves that nothing has changed, that primeval war goes on. Man is capable of love and hate, murder and sacrifice. He is

Abraham and Isaac together. God Himself hasn't changed." I was angry.

"After what happened to us, how can you believe in God?" With an understanding smile on his lips, the Rebbe answered:

"How can you not believe in God after what happened?"

The two adults were not longer alive. Their tongues hung swollen, blue tinged. But the third rope was still moving; being so light, the child was still alive. For more than half an hour he stayed there, struggling between life and death, dying slow agony under our eyes. And we had to look him in the face. He was still alive when I passed in front of him. His tongue was still red, his eyes not yet glazed. Behind me I heard a voice saying, "Where is God now?" And I heard a voice within me answer him: "Where is He? Here He is — hanging."

"Oh God, be with me when I have need of you, but above all, do not leave me when I deny you."

...CONSTERNATION...

I wonder. Those who entered the gas chambers with the praise of God on their lips are often ridiculed for their passivity and faith. But were they at least free in their deaths? The Germans were to destroy their bodies, but recognizing that, they determined that their souls were to belong forever to the Master of the World. But so what? The Nazis could have cared less about the singing — it would end soon enough. What meaning, then, could there be in their deaths?

I wonder. Did we as Jews survive because of these who believed, or do we owe our lives to those who either despaired or rebelled immediately, to those who had neither faith or patience for the future?

I wonder. Was the Holocaust one of God's tests from which He in His great mercy allowed us to emerge because of those among our parents who remained faithful? Or do we breathe today because some of our parents had the courage to become indignant at God's constant testing of His people?

I wonder. Perhaps it was a punishment, in which God, as our

father, got carried away, His wrath turning His beating into a killing. Then did we escape death because of those who were willing to trust in their Father until He came to His senses? Or because of those who determined that He had gone mad and decided to run away from Him?

If it were a test, what was He testing? Our insistence on remaining as faithful as did Job when everything around us encouraged distrust? Our ability to remain sane amidst madness? Our capacity for love when hatred rained down upon us? Our tenacity for compassion in the face of bitterness? Our desire to remain Jewish while witnessing the genocide of our people? What kind of a God would devise such a test? What kind of God would want a people who could pass it? What kind of a people needs such a God?

And if it were a punishment? For what were we being punished? Not following all the 613 commandments of a God who had not spoken to His people for thousands of years? Not being able to understand Massada, the Crusades, the Inquisition, or the Pogroms? Not returning to Zion because we were awaiting the coming of the Messiah? Not all being Rabbi Akiba's, Bar Kochba's, or Herzl's? Not remaining distinct from a society into which we had been sent because He had allowed the destruction of the Second Temple for reasons of His own? What kind of God would be so non-understanding as to create such punishment? What kind of God would want a people who had to be so punished? What kind of a people need such a God?

...AND CONFIRMATION

> I believe in the sun when it is not shining,
> I believe in love even when feeling it not,
> I believe in God even when He is silent.
>
> —Written anonomously on the wall of
> a cellar hideout during the Holocaust.

One who believed even as she was living through this Hell on Earth was Anne Frank. We do not know what her final thoughts were on the way to the gas chamber, but her words recorded in a diary kept during her years in hiding offer eternal inspiration:

> I don't think then of all the misery, but of the beauty that still remains. There is one of the things that Mummy and I are so entirely different about. Her counsel when one feels melancholy

is: "Think of all the misery in the world and be thankful you're not sharing in it!" My advice is: "Go outside, to the fields, enjoy nature and the sunshine, go out and try to recapture happiness in yourself and God. Think of all the beauty that's still left in and around you and be happy."

I don't know how Mummy's idea can be right, because then how are you supposed to behave if you go through the misery yourself? Then you are lost. On the contrary, I've found that there is always some beauty left — in nature, sunshine, freedom, in yourself; these can all help you. Look at these things, then find yourself again, and God, and then you can regain your balance . . .

It's really a wonder that I haven't dropped all my ideals, because they seem so absurd and impossible to carry out. Yet I keep them, because in spite of everything I still believe that people are really good at heart. I simply can't build my hopes on a foundation of confusion, misery and death. I see the world gradually being turned into a wilderness. I hear the approaching thunder, I can feel the suffering of millions, and yet, if I look up into the heavens, I think that it will all come out right one of these days, that this cruelty will end, and that peace and tranquility will return again. In the meantime, I must hold on to my ideals, for perhaps the day will come when I shall be able to carry them out.

It is an unsettling thought, to think of Anne Frank naked, dead and rotting among the corpses in the pits at Bergen-Belsen. Yet that is what the Holocaust is; that thought, multiplied six million times.

Eric A. Kimmel

A Song

SAKHAKI, SAKHAKI

Sakhaki, sakhaki al hakhalomot,
Zu ani hakhalom sakh,
Sakhaki ki va-adam a-amin,
Ki ohdeni ma-amin bakh.

Ki od nafshi d'ror sho-efet
Lo m'kharti-ah l'eygel paz,
Ki od a-amin gam ba-adam,
Gam b'rukho, ruakh az.

A-aminah gam be-atid,
Af im yirkhak zeh hayom.
Af bo yavo — yisoo shalom
Az uv'rakha l'om mil'om.

שחקי , שחקי
שחקי , שחקי על החלומות ,
זו אני החולם שח ,
שחקי כי באדם אאמין ,
כי עודני מאמין בך .

כי עוד נפשי דרור שואפת
לא מכרתיה לעגל פז ,
כי עוד אאמין גם באדם ,
גם ברוחו , רוח עז .

אאמינה גם בעתיד ,
אף אם ירחק זה היום .
אך בא יבוא – ישאו שלום
אז וברכה לאם מלאם .

Smile, friend, smile away my dreams!
What I dream shall yet come true!
Smile that I believe in man,
As I still believe in you.

My soul still yearns for liberty,
Unbartered for a calf of gold;
For still I do believe in man,
And in his spirit, strong and bold.

And in the future I believe —
Though it be distant, come it will —
When nations shall each other bless
And peace at last the earth shall fill.

— S. Tchernikovsky
© by the author

84

Fill this page with dots. How close do you come to 6,000,000? Now imagine each one the size of a person, a relative, even — alive.

יד מרדכי
Yad Mordecai

think Although the foundations for a Jewish State were certainly laid much earlier, the murder of one-third of the world's Jews appears to have been a final event leading to the legal establishment of Israel. Yad Mordecai seems better than many places to crystallize some of the relationship between the two events — one so catastrophic and the other so magnificent.

read Seeing the battlefield and walking through the museum here was really .... A place like this makes it clear that people fleeing Nazi Europe were .... , ...

What might have been if more had been able to get out? If Israel had existed before Hitler? Here is one place . . .

And thinking about it all, Israel . . .

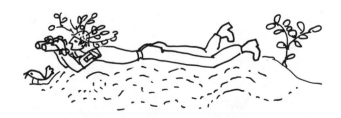

connect Shmulik Koiler, a defender of the kibbutz who had earlier wanted to evacuate the settlement was now glad they hadn't, as he watched the enemy tank roll evenly toward them. He shouted to his companions about having to stop it, and with grenades in both his hands, he ran straight toward the armored vehicle.

He tossed the grenades and they found their mark, exploding directly in front of the machine gun slit — but not before the Egyptian gunner had managed to swing the tank's turret around and fire. The tank stopped cold and three Egyptians scrambled out and fled back to the fence. But they were forgotten for the moment, as Shmulik, who had fallen — almost cut in half by the tank's bullets — now writhed in agony and screamed for someone to kill him.

But someone else was screaming too, trying to direct the attention of those defenders still capable of fighting towards the fence from which fresh enemy fighters were now attacking, firing as they came.

Zvi spun around and shot at them. Two dropped and the rest fled. Then, turning back to Shmulik, he was hit by a bullet in the forehead and killed. Someone else had to put an end to Shmulik's torturous suffering.[4]

know Yad Mordechai, a *Hashomer Hatzair* (left-wing socialist) kibbutz, is located in southern Israel between Ashkelon and the Gaza Strip. Founded in 1943, during the Holocaust, by a group fleeing Poland, it is named after Mordechai Anielewicz, one of the contingent's friends who was killed as a leader in the Warsaw ghetto uprising.

During the War of Liberation (1947-8) the kibbutz came under heavy attack by the Egyptian army. Although eventually overrun, the kibbutzniks were able to hold off the enemy long enough to allow for crucial fortification of areas further north on the way to Tel Aviv. Retaken in October 1948, the kibbutz has since been rebuilt, and now contains a museum of Holocaust and ghetto resistance, and a life-size reconstruction of the battle that was fought there.

Yad Mordecai

From Holocaust . . . to Statehood . . .

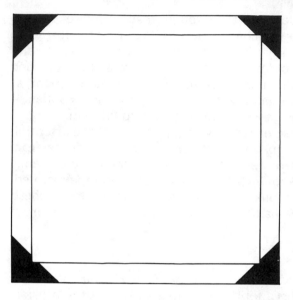

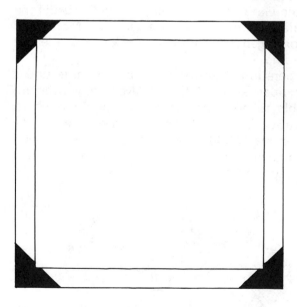

עכו
Acco

think The War of Liberation (1947-8) was a hard battle won by ideals, courage, and a belief in self-determination. Many of Israel's finest soldiers, doctors, lawyers, farmers, teachers, and others lost their lives, but not always on the battlefields. The resistance that went on everywhere, even amongst the Jewish prisoners in the British jails (with the hanging room positioned right next to the cells), was nothing less than heroic.

read I went to Acco the other day. It's an old fortress from Crusader times, but more recently, just twenty-five years ago, it was used as a British prison and held many of the Jewish freedom fighters, some of whom were actually hanged there during the pre-state period. The things that struck me the most about the place were . . .

connect Menachem Begin, leader of the "Irgun Tzvai Leumi" (ארגון צבאי לאומי—*Etzel*), received the following letter from one of his soldiers being held in the British prison in Acco:

. . . Of course I want to live; but what pains me, now that the end is so near, is mainly the awareness that I have not succeeded in achieving enough . . . I could have

enjoyed life and been contented with the job I was promised on my demobilization. I could even have left the country altogether for a safer life in America, but this would not have satisfied me either as a Jew or as a Zionist.

There are many schools of thought as to how a Jew should choose his way of life. One way is that of the assimilationists who have renounced their Jewishness. There is also another way, the way of those who call themselves 'Zionists' - the way of negotiation and compromise, as if the existence of a nation were but another transaction. They are not prepared to make any sacrifice, and therefore they have to make concessions and accept compromises. Perhaps this is a means of delaying the end, but, in the final analysis, it leads to the ghetto . . .

The only way that seems, to my mind, to be right, is the way of the Irgun Tzvai Leumi, the way of courage and daring without renouncing a single inch of our homeland. When political negotiations prove futile, one must be prepared to fight for our homeland and our freedom. Without them the very existence of our nation is jeopardized, so fight we must with all possible means. This is the only way left to our people in their hour of decision: to stand on our rights, to be ready to fight, even if for some of us this way leads to the gallows. For it is a law of history that only with blood shall a country be redeemed.

I am writing this while awaiting the hangman. This is not a moment at which I can lie, and I swear that if I had to begin my life anew I would have chosen the same way, regardless of the consequences for myself.

Dov Gruner

know Dov Gruner was hanged on the gallows of the Acco prison on April 16, 1947, shortly after the above letter was sent. Although his militant views were representative of only a minority of Palestine's Jews (the majority subscribing to the Haganah's more moderate approach), the courage they demonstrate are reflective of the mood of the people at the time. Shortly after his death his fellow prisoners executed a daring escape from the jail, undermining the British claim of tight control over Palestine. The citadel has since been turned into a museum of national martyrdom in their collective honor — and in memory of the eight prisoners who were hanged there.

Historically, Acco (or Acre) is one of the oldest trade towns in the world, having served as one of the borders of the tribe of Asher in Biblical times, as a port city for the Greeks in the 3rd century BCE, as a Jewish fishing village during the time of the Roman conquest, and as a Crusader fortress in the 13th century. It was restored by the Turks in the 1700s, and only when the British were granted the Mandate over Palestine (following WWI), did the city begin to lose its commercial importance. It exists today in the shadow of Haifa, situated across the bay.

Crusaders fortress . . . and British prison . . .

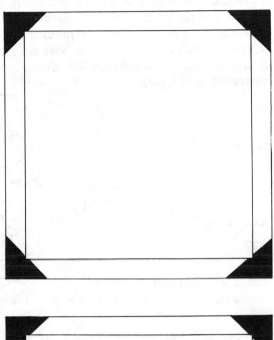

Crypto-Gram

Start figuring out what the 44 words described below are. When you've got some of them, begin to fill in the Crypto-Gram board. How? The numbers under each letter of the words you define, correspond to the numbers in the blank spaces of the puzzle. Going from board to blanks, and back and forth, you will eventually end up with a headache. Shortly thereafter you should end up with an important quotation from a famous Zionist thinker — if you're lucky. If you're not lucky, the answers can be found on p.246. All in all, a good compilation of thoughts on oppression, struggle, resistance, and return.

DEFINITIONS

a.

$\overline{224}$ $\overline{84}$ $\overline{145}$ $\overline{165}$ $\overline{177}$ $\overline{97}$

early pioneers who came to Israel from Russia in 1882

b.

$\overline{27}$ $\overline{201}$ $\overline{175}$ $\overline{75}$ $\overline{22}$ $\quad$ $\overline{160}$ $\overline{91}$ $\overline{269}$ $\overline{194}$ $\overline{9}$

first modern Jewish settlement in Palestine

c.

$\overline{192}$ $\overline{55}$ $\overline{171}$ $\overline{146}$ $\overline{235}$ $\overline{211}$ $\overline{40}$ $\overline{223}$ $\overline{35}$

worst nightmare ever to come upon Jews in #aa below

d.

$\overline{138}$ $\overline{121}$ $\overline{87}$ $\overline{17}$ $\overline{139}$ $\overline{255}$ $\overline{70}$

location of episode of Jewish resistance against Roman domination

e.

$\overline{224}$ $\overline{94}$ $\overline{124}$ $\overline{239}$ $\overline{163}$ $\overline{39}$ $\overline{86}$ $\overline{143}$ $\overline{253}$

location of the first Exile

f.

$\overline{1}$ $\overline{265}$ $\overline{108}$ $\overline{53}$ $\overline{21}$

land from which Moses led the enslaved Jews

g. $\overline{32}\ \overline{37}\ \overline{123}\ \overline{81}\ \overline{97}\ \overline{56}\ \overline{16}\ \overline{159}\ \overline{207}\ \overline{233}$
the age to be brought by #11

h. $\overline{8}\ \overline{48}\ \overline{240}\ \overline{226}\ \overline{187}\ \overline{257}$
the law of this name assures all Jews citizenship rights in Israel

i. $\overline{266}\ \overline{46}\ \overline{249}\ \overline{177}\ \overline{111}\ \overline{183}\ \overline{271}\ \overline{122}$
one component of Judaism, the other of which is nationality

j. $\overline{156}\ \overline{67}\ \overline{232}\ \overline{108}\ \overline{3}\ \overline{179}$
dialogue between God and man that has kept Jews going for centuries

k. $\overline{44}\ \overline{10}\ \overline{41}\ \quad \overline{170}\ \overline{90}\ \overline{12}\ \overline{149}$
the first all Jewish city in the world since Jerusalem was destroyed

l. $\overline{34}\ \overline{70}\ \overline{89}\ \overline{30}\ \overline{61}\ \overline{215}\ \quad \overline{124}\ \overline{104}\ \overline{224}\ \overline{141}\ \overline{29}$
modern Jewish philosopher; authored *I and Thou*

m. $\overline{140}\ \overline{216}\ \overline{129}\ \overline{189}\ \overline{228}\ \overline{117}\ \overline{158}\ \quad \overline{22}\ \overline{20}\ \overline{247}\ \overline{176}\ \overline{11}$
father of the Jewish state

n. $\overline{115}\ \overline{18}\ \overline{231}\ \overline{142}\ \overline{78}\ \overline{97}$
term for massacres and pillaging of East European Jews at turn of century

o. $\overline{88}\ \overline{65}\ \overline{180}\ \overline{63}\ \overline{203}\ \overline{50}\ \overline{27}\ \overline{253}\ \overline{212}\ \overline{59}\ \overline{214}\ \overline{264}$
the period when Europe's Jews were granted equality

p. $\overline{200}\ \overline{267}\ \overline{74}\ \overline{216}\ \overline{58}\ \overline{123}\ \overline{179}\ \overline{72}\ \overline{210}$
ancient Jewish court that Napolean tried to revive for #o

q.

$\overline{219}$ $\overline{196}$ $\overline{259}$ $\overline{248}$ $\overline{31}$ $\overline{113}$ $\overline{13}$

reaction to his trial in France in 1895 inspired #m

r.

$\overline{93}$ $\overline{36}$ $\overline{174}$ $\overline{4}$ $\overline{127}$ $\overline{15}$

cluttered Jewish communities of which Warsaw is the most famous

s.

$\overline{66}$ $\overline{14}$ $\overline{76}$ $\overline{23}$ $\overline{25}$ $\overline{216}$ $\overline{188}$ $\overline{252}$ $\overline{69}$ $\overline{19}$ $\overline{204}$ $\overline{100}$ $\overline{60}$

period which brought on #o

t.

$\overline{34}$ $\overline{9}$ $\overline{230}$ $\overline{32}$ $\overline{186}$ $\overline{24}$ $\overline{33}$ $\overline{7}$

Spanish Jews who during Inquisition professed Christianity

u.

$\overline{79}$ $\overline{45}$ $\overline{211}$ $\overline{163}$ $\overline{229}$ $\overline{138}$

hello and goodby in Hebrew; the dream of the Jews

v.

$\overline{261}$ $\overline{204}$ $\overline{147}$ $\quad$ $\overline{224}$ $\overline{218}$ $\overline{173}$ $\overline{112}$ $\overline{203}$ $\overline{22}$ $\overline{205}$ $\overline{167}$

socialist Zionist Jew who lived 1881-1917

w.

$\overline{43}$ $\overline{196}$ $\overline{172}$ $\overline{198}$ $\overline{123}$ $\overline{102}$ $\overline{97}$

one of the things the *Pesach Seder* celebrates

x.

$\overline{203}$ $\overline{209}$ $\overline{165}$ $\overline{80}$ $\overline{139}$ $\overline{123}$ $\overline{54}$ $\overline{82}$

11th century Christian campaigns to conquer Holy Land

y.

$\overline{49}$ $\overline{75}$ $\overline{260}$ $\quad$ $\overline{64}$ $\overline{107}$

$\overline{145}$ $\overline{109}$ $\overline{224}$ $\overline{98}$ $\overline{114}$ $\overline{9}$ $\overline{136}$ $\overline{132}$ $\overline{85}$ $\overline{202}$

Israel's fight for independence

z.

$\overline{144}$ $\overline{92}$ $\overline{243}$ $\overline{50}$ - $\overline{38}$ $\overline{116}$ $\overline{34}$ $\overline{59}$ $\overline{191}$ $\overline{23}$ $\overline{95}$ $\overline{19}$

continuous hatred of the Jews

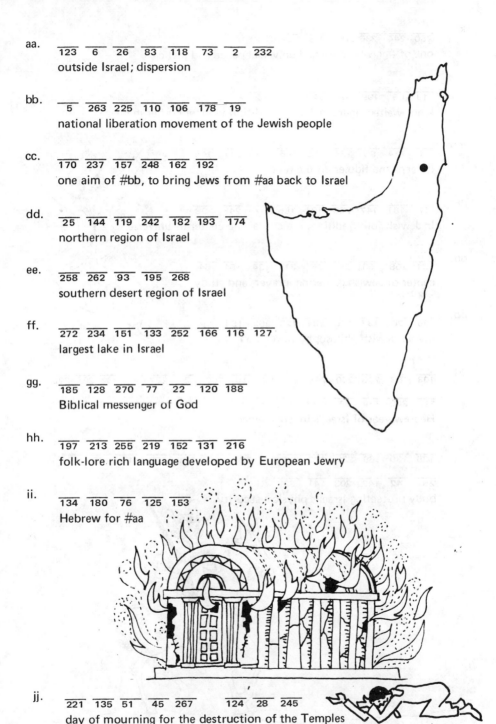

aa.

$\overline{123}$ $\overline{6}$ $\overline{26}$ $\overline{83}$ $\overline{118}$ $\overline{73}$ $\overline{2}$ $\overline{232}$

outside Israel; dispersion

bb.

$\overline{5}$ $\overline{263}$ $\overline{225}$ $\overline{110}$ $\overline{106}$ $\overline{178}$ $\overline{19}$

national liberation movement of the Jewish people

cc.

$\overline{170}$ $\overline{237}$ $\overline{157}$ $\overline{248}$ $\overline{162}$ $\overline{192}$

one aim of #bb, to bring Jews from #aa back to Israel

dd.

$\overline{25}$ $\overline{144}$ $\overline{119}$ $\overline{242}$ $\overline{182}$ $\overline{193}$ $\overline{174}$

northern region of Israel

ee.

$\overline{258}$ $\overline{262}$ $\overline{93}$ $\overline{195}$ $\overline{268}$

southern desert region of Israel

ff.

$\overline{272}$ $\overline{234}$ $\overline{151}$ $\overline{133}$ $\overline{252}$ $\overline{166}$ $\overline{116}$ $\overline{127}$

largest lake in Israel

gg.

$\overline{185}$ $\overline{128}$ $\overline{270}$ $\overline{77}$ $\overline{22}$ $\overline{120}$ $\overline{188}$

Biblical messenger of God

hh.

$\overline{197}$ $\overline{213}$ $\overline{255}$ $\overline{219}$ $\overline{152}$ $\overline{131}$ $\overline{216}$

folk-lore rich language developed by European Jewry

ii.

$\overline{134}$ $\overline{180}$ $\overline{76}$ $\overline{125}$ $\overline{153}$

Hebrew for #aa

jj.

$\overline{221}$ $\overline{135}$ $\overline{51}$ $\overline{45}$ $\overline{267}$ $\overline{124}$ $\overline{28}$ $\overline{245}$

day of mourning for the destruction of the Temples

kk. $\overline{250}$ $\overline{244}$ $\overline{236}$ $\overline{168}$ $\overline{96}$ $\overline{36}$

one of #gg who preached universal peace and justice

ll. $\overline{19}$ $\overline{68}$ $\overline{199}$ $\overline{184}$ $\overline{220}$ $\overline{232}$ $\overline{52}$

long awaited figure in Jewish tradition who will usher in peace

mm. $\overline{71}$ $\overline{114}$ $\overline{99}$ $\overline{228}$ $\overline{222}$ $\overline{126}$ $\overline{256}$ $\overline{241}$ $\overline{105}$

it keeps the fiddler on the roof

nn. $\overline{47}$ $\overline{181}$ $\overline{147}$ $\overline{208}$ $\overline{101}$ $\overline{186}$ $\overline{57}$ $\overline{246}$ $\overline{138}$

in Jewish folk-tradition, the city at the center of universe

oo. $\overline{131}$ $\overline{108}$ $\overline{63}$ $\overline{28}$ $\overline{25}$ $\overline{217}$ $\overline{134}$ $\overline{161}$ $\overline{54}$

center of Jewish gathering, prayer, and study

pp. $\overline{36}$ $\overline{28}$ $\overline{137}$ $\overline{155}$ $\overline{234}$ $\overline{123}$ $\overline{263}$ $\overline{154}$ $\overline{19}$

joyous Jewish philosophy of religion

qq. $\overline{103}$ $\overline{183}$ $\overline{206}$ $\overline{240}$ $\overline{248}$ $\quad$ $\overline{164}$ $\overline{10}$ $\overline{169}$ $\overline{3}$ $\overline{227}$ $\quad$ $\overline{232}$ $\overline{254}$ $\overline{228}$

$\overline{193}$ $\overline{250}$ $\overline{134}$ $\overline{22}$ $\overline{212}$

Hebrew year of Israel's independence

rr. $\overline{135}$ $\overline{130}$ $\overline{166}$ $\overline{236}$ $\overline{148}$ $\overline{238}$ $\quad$ $\overline{228}$ $\overline{246}$ $\overline{190}$ $\overline{150}$ $\overline{14}$ $\overline{235}$ $\overline{46}$

$\overline{251}$ $\overline{42}$ $\overline{142}$ $\overline{203}$ $\overline{141}$ $\overline{62}$

body protecting Israel's physical security

Crypto-Gram Board

1 f	2 aa	3 j	4 r	5 bb		6 aa	7 r	8 n	9 b	10 k	11 m		12 k	13 q		14 s	15 r	16 g
17 d	18 n	19 s	20 m	21 f	22 b	23 s	24 t	25 dd		26 aa	27 b	28 jj	29 l	30 l		31 q	32 g	33 t	34 l
35 c	36 r	37 g		38 z	39 e	40 c	41 k		42 rr	43 w		44 k	45 u	46 i		47 nn	48 h	49 y	—
50 o	51 jj	52 ll		53 f	54 oo	55 c	56 g	57 nn	58 p / J		59 o	60 s		61 l	62 rr		63 o	64 y
65 o	66 s	67 j	68 ll		69 s	70 l	71 mm	72 p	73 aa	74 p	75 b	76 s		77 gg	78 n	79 u	—
80 x	81 g	82 x	83 aa	84 a	85 y	86 e ,		87 d	88 o	89 l	90 k	91 b	92 z	93 r		94 e	95 z
96 kk		97 a	98 y	99 mm	100 s	101 nn		102 w	103 qq		104 l	105 mm	106 bb	107 y	108 f	109 y	110 bb	111 i
112 v	113 q	114 y		115 n	116 z	117 m	118 aa	119 dd	120 gg		121 d	122 i	123 g		124 s	125 ii	126 mm	—
127 r	128 gg	129 m	130 rr	131 hh	132 y	133 ff	134 ii		135 jj	136 y	137 pp		138 d	139 d	140 m	141 l	142 n	143 e	—
144 z	145 a	)	146 c	147 v		148 rr	149 k	150 rr	151 ff		152 hh	153 ii	154 pp		155 pp	156 j	157 cc	—
158 m	159 g	160 b	161 oo	162 cc	163 e ,		164 qq	165 a	166 ff	167 v	168 kk	169 qq	170 k	171 c	
172 w	173 v	174 r	175 b	176 m		177 a	178 bb	179 p	180 c	181 nn	182 dd		183 i	184 ll		185 gg	186 t	187 h	188 s
189 m	190 rr		191 z	192 c	193 dd		194 b	195 ee	196 q	197 hh		198 w	199 ll	200 p	201 b	202 y	203 o	204 s
205 v	206 qq		207 g	208 nn	209 x		210 p	211 c	212 o	213 hh	214 o	215 l	216 m	217 oo	218 v	219 q	.
220 ll	221 jj		222 mm	223 c		224 a	225 bb	226 h	227 qq	228 m		229 u	230 t	231 n	232 j	233 g	234 ff	—
235 c	236 kk	237 cc	238 rr	239 e		240 h	241 mm		242 dd	243 z	244 kk		245 jj	246 nn	247 m	248 q
249 i	250 kk	251 rr	252 s		253 e	254 qq	255 d		256 mm	257 h	258 ee	259 q	260 y		261 v	262 ee	263 bb	264 o	265 f
—	266 i	267 p	268 ee		269 b	270 gg	271 i	272 ff										

(1 8 6 5 — 1 9 3 5)

Extra help: the letter printed in the lower right hand corner of each empty box refers to the word you've got to define in order to discover the missing letter.

A Thought

There is a supreme effort demanded of the Jew by the creation of the State of Israel. For the first time in centuries the Jewish people has secured a base from which to create a truly Jewish way of doing things. With total control over all the institutions concerned — educational, social, cultural, political, economic, and military — there exists now, after a gap of almost 2000 years, the opportunity to take up again a living struggle with the meaning of Jewish existence. All of the spiritual strivings and national aspirations — focused for so long in the abstract — are suddenly presented with a concrete foundation from which to materialize and mature.

But what is to be done with them? So long has Judaism been consistently and automatically referred to as "a way of life" that the phrase has become infested with triteness. Oftentimes it deludes us into the misconception that we are dismissed from having to determine exactly what it means. Or perhaps, before the creation of the State, such discussion seemed absurdly theoretical. In any case, it is this generation of Jews that has become obligated to the generations of our forefathers. We have been placed into a confrontation with rhetoric, the challenge, or maybe pinnacle test of creating a dynamic reality out of otherwise empty phrases. The individual Jew must come to accept the responsibility — and become exhilirated by the opportunity — to help evolve a dynamism in Judaism heretofore unknown.

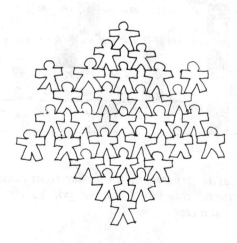

Section 5
THE SOUL

שלות
שלום

Between God & Man

A uniquely Jewish expression of the yearnings, fears, dreams, and wonder that all humanity experiences, the *Siddur* (סדור), or traditional prayerbook, is to us one of Judaism's most beautiful texts. Through it we can feel a communality with our fellow Jews throughout time and throughout space, and through it we can come to appreciate how a relationship with the physical world around us can help us to discover the spiritual implications of our being here. A quick look at three excerpts from the morning prayers (שחרית) provides an example.

Thanking God for providing us with everything necessary is one of the first orders of business:

Blessed are you, Lord our God, King of the universe, who has made for me all that I need.

ברוך אתה ה'
אלוהנו מלך העולם
שעשה לי כל
צרכי.

Not that we always feel this way, but perhaps that's because we don't know how to take advantage of, and exploit, all that there really is in the world. Maybe discovering how to do that comes along with discovering God. And that, we promise ourselves, is a process open to us all:

God is close to all who call on Him, to all who call on Him in truth.

קרוב ה'
לכל קוראיו,
לכל אשר
יקראוהו באמת.

If it doesn't seem that way sometimes, maybe it's because the meaning of "in truth" has evaded us.

Maybe, just maybe, we don't use all of our being, or don't apply all that we might to the effort. Still, we assure ourselves that everyday we may uncover something new which will help us learn how to:

And (God) in His goodness continually renews every day the act of creation.

ובטובו מחדש בכל יום
תמיד מעשה בראשית

If we've missed something until now, we have another chance tomorrow. Thank God.

Especially now that you're in Israel, pick up a prayerbook and explore. Who knows, you might somehow feel closer to it all being here; so many of our prayers and psalms were inspired by the Jew's sense of mystery with even the physical phenomena of his world in *Eretz Yisrael*. So strong was this physical consciousness that even though we lived in Exile for almost 2000 years, we nevertheless prayed for rain and dew according to the seasonal changes in *Eretz Yisrael*, and not in the lands of our sojournings. And throughout the ages, whenever we prayed, our hearts were warmed by the activation of our 3000 year old love affair with Jerusalem.

But as much as the prayerbook is part of Jewish tradition, so is the individual's personal prayer. And that no one can write for anyone else. No one can even know what form it should take. Silence, song, liturgy, chanting, and swaying are only a few of the ways of . . . well, praying. It's not only the form that counts; it's the inside part too:

the recognition of the everyday amazing things, and the coming to terms with the not so amazing ones;

the appreciation of some of the metaphysical dimensions of living, and the responsible relating to life's very real obstacles;

the struggling to communicate with God, and the persistence in seeking out some hint of that All-Encompassing-Whatever when only nothingness seems to respond instead.

"Prayer is a universal phenomenon in the soul-life of man. It is the soul's reaction to the terrors and joys, the uncertainties and dreams of life. 'The reason why we pray,' says William James, 'is simply that we cannot help praying.' "

Following are a few examples of what a number of others couldn't help but say. Some may be outside traditional Jewish frameworks. Some may be right for you, some may not. But they've worked for others neither more nor less qualified than any of us to offer a personal prayer.

Let your prayer be a window to heaven.
The Ba'al Shem Tov

i thank you God for most this amazing
day: for the leaping greenly spirit of trees
and a blue true dream of sky; and for everything
which is natural which is infinite which is yes

(i who have died am alive again today,
and this is the sun's birthday; this is the birth
day of life and of love and wings: and of the gay
great happening illimitably earth)

how should tasting touching hearing seeing
breathing any — lifted from the no
of all nothing — human merely being
doubt unimaginable you?

(now the ears of my ears awake and
now the eyes of my eyes are opened)

e.e. cummings

You should utter words as though Heaven were
opened within them, and as though you did not
put the word in your mouth, but as though
you entered into the word.
Hassidic saying

Now let me tell you about a devoted but simple Jew who made his living by driving a horse and wagon, delivering people and packages around the countryside. He didn't know the traditional prayers, but every day he would reaffirm his love for God by saying: "God, if you ever wanted to go anywhere, or ever wanted me to take anything someplace for you, know that I'd do it happily, without taking a thing in exchange. I'd do it out of devotion." Well, he never had the opportunity to prove it, but trust me, he meant what he said.

One day one of his passengers was a rather well-known rabbi, and, if you'll excuse my saying so, a bit of a self-righteous one too. And, as they were driving along, this rabbi overheard the prayer of the driver and burst out angrily: "Fool, that's not the way to pray. You're insulting the Almighty with that nonsense!" The simple man, wishing only to please God, and naturally respecting the position of his traveller, asked him how, then, he should pray. The scholar proceeded to use the rest of the journey to teach him the proper blessings, and, when he got out at his destination, was rather satisfied with himself for having saved this ignorant soul.

As for the driver, it had all happened too fast, and, once without his teacher, he quickly forgot the formal liturgy. But now, as you might well imagine, he was also afraid to address God as he used to. So he kept his feelings inside and said nothing.

> There is no room for God in one who
> is full of himself
> — The Baal Shem Tov

But feelings too can rise upwards, and when these were carried to God he was not so pleased with the rabbi as the rabbi was with himself. That very night he visited him in a dream, and reproached him, saying: "Return to the driver and tell him that his old prayer is all I desire. And know that in the meantime you have interrupted the dialogue between Myself and one of My most faithful believers."

The rabbi, I assure you, wasted no time in seeking out the fellow. And when he found him he lowered his eyes in shame, and said: "It is you who are the teacher and I who am the simple man. Continue in your old prayer, for it is not words, but sincerity, that God desires."

— Based on a traditional Jewish folktale

> When wood burns, it is only the smoke that rises;
> the grosser elements are left below. With prayer,
> it is the same thing; only the sincere feelings
> ascend to heaven. — The Ba'al Shem Tov

Praise me, says God, and I will know that you love me.
Curse me, says God, and I will know that you love me.
Praise me or curse me
And I will know that you love me.

Sing out my graces, says God.
Raise your fist against me and revile, says God.
Sing out graces or revile
Revile is also a kind of praise, says God.

But if you sit fenced off in your apathy, says God,
If you sit entrenched in: "I don't give a damn," says God,
If you look at the stars and yawn,
If you see suffering and don't cry out,
If you don't praise and you don't revile,
Then I created you in vain, says God.

—.Aharon Zeitlin
(translated by Emanuel Goldsmith)

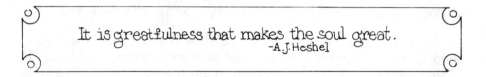

It is greatfulness that makes the soul great.
-A.J.Heshel

A Jewish folktale concerns a small inarticulate Jewish shepherd boy who stood outside of the synagogue and listened, enraptured, to the chanting of the prayers inside. The boy entered, drawn by the intensity of feeling, and stood awestruck among the worshippers. He yearned to open his lips and offer a prayer to God, but because he was unable to speak, he could only stand in silence as others around him prayed with great devotion.

An overwhelming desire to join with the others took hold of the boy, and he opened his lips in an attempt to form a sound, any sound. A piercing whistle broke forth from his lips, and his face lit up ecstatically as he whistled his praises to God.

Astonished, the worshippers stopped their chanting; whistling in the synagogue was unheard of. They turned to the rabbi, expecting him to reprimand the youngster.

The rabbi knew the boy well, and with tears in his eyes, approached him, "My boy, don't be frightened. God desires prayer

which comes from the heart and soul, and your prayer is among the most beautiful God has ever heard."
— Based on a traditional Jewish folktale

The Tzaner Rabbi was asked by a Hasid: "What do you do before praying?"
"I pray," was the reply, "that I may be able to pray properly."

your turn

During this time spent in Israel a lot of things are happening around you, some of them probably rather heavy. Here's a section in which you can write down some special thought or feeling or poem in reaction to it all. When we say it's a place to write your own prayer, we don't necessarily mean to speak to God; as far as we know, you might not even believe in Him. But regardless, take a few moments to reflect: on Israel ... on the people you've met ... on the things you've seen ... on the history you've uncovered ... on the ways you've been feeling ...

Need some inspiration? Glance at the old city of Jerusalem in the distance, or at the majesty of the snow-capped peak of the Hermon, or at the silent beauty of the Negev at sunset, or at the lush greenery of the Galilee at dawn. And concentrate on feeling that here, **here**, is where that conversation between *Am Yisrael*, *Eretz Yisrael*, and *Torat Yisrael* is taking place — and that inside of you an urge to join in begins to stir. Don't be shy,

"God is no less here than there. It is the sacred moment in which His presence is disclosed. We meet God in time rather than in space. The history of Jerusalem is endowed with the power to inspire such moments, to invoke in us the ability to be present in His presence."
— A.J. Heschel

That Jews have for centuries placed scraps of paper inscribed with their most profound prayers into the crevices of the *Kotel*, is a physical manifestation of the individual's need to express his unity with all of the Jewish past when dealing with the present and encountering the future.

Give it a try. *"There is cursing in the world, scheming, and very little praying. Let Jerusalem inspire praying: an end to rage, an end to violence."*
— A.J. Heschel

People To People

"And what is a friend? More than a father, more than a brother. A traveling companion. With him you can conquer the impossible, even if you must lose it later. Friendship marks a life even more deeply than love. Love risks degenerating into obsession. Friendship is never anything but sharing. It is to a friend that you can communicate the awakening of a desire, the birth of a vision or a terror, the anguish of seeing the sun disappear, or of finding that order and justice are no more. What is a friend? Someone who for the first time makes you aware of your loneliness and of his, and helps you escape so you in turn can help him. Thanks to him you can hold your tongue without shame or talk freely without risk."

— Elie Wiesel

Do not separate yourself from the community...
In the place where there are no men
strive to be a man.
—Pirke Avot

Part of the soul of Israel is the people of Israel. Integral to the life style of *Am Yisrael* is the concept of community: *"Jerusalem is not divine, her life depends on our presence. Alone she is a widow; with Israel she is a bride."*

— A.J. Heschel

107

The two were sitting next to each other on an Egged bus on the way to Jerusalem, and got involved in small talk. "Do you know Moshe Goldman?"

"Do I know Moshe Goldman? Of course I know Moishele!"

"What kind of person is he?"

"Must you ask? He's as stubborn as a mule. One who didn't know him could easily get the idea that he was really a somebody. But it takes someone a lot cleverer than Moishele to fool me!"

"What do you really know about him?"

"Hoh! What I know about him? What I know about him! What will you say for instance if I tell you that he borrows money and never returns it. He trades on the black market. He beats his wife. He rides on Shabbat. He even eats on Yom Kippur!"

"But how do you know all these things about him?"

"What do you mean 'how do I know?' Moishele is my very best friend!"

— Based on a traditional Jewish folktale

> The spirit of God delights in he who does good to his fellowman.
>
> —Pirke Avot

The Roots Of Shabbat[5]

"The solution of mankind's most vexing problem will not be found in renouncing technical civilization, but in attaining some degree of independence of it . . . The Sabbath is the day on which we learn the art of **surpassing** *civilization."*

— A.J. Heschel

Shabbat allows us a day of harmony: between man and man, man and the world, and man and God. It is a day to minimize the frustrations of the superficial conflicts of our daily lives, and to concentrate instead on the interrelation of all things natural. This most important holiday, then, not only reminds us of the creation story, but encompasses as well that deep connection between *Am Yisrael, Eretz Yisrael,* and *Torat Yisrael* — a tie that binds a **land,** a **people,** and a **book.**

It's common knowledge that we celebrate Shabbat because God created the world in six days and rested on the seventh, but only some realize as well that Shabbat is also a commemoration of the Exodus from Egypt.

In ancient times, weather and climate often caused draught in Canaan, where the Jews were living. Just to the southwest, however, was Egypt with her fertile Nile River Basin. Migration between the two areas was therefore common, and for many years the Jewish people even lived permanently among the Egyptians in order to take advantage of the better agricultural situation to be found there. For political reasons they were eventually enslaved, and it wasn't until Moses came along that it became clear that, as the Bible tells us, God initiated a process which would eventually lead to their freedom.

But unable to think as free men, and thus still dependent on tangible guardians for their needs, the Jews were consequently unable to believe wholeheartedly in an invisible God, regardless of the deeds attributed to Him. Their being physically lost, though recorded as punishment for their incomplete faith, seems to us to be symbolic as well of their mental disorientation. It takes a long time for a people used to living as slaves to start thinking for themselves as responsible for their own lives. To our minds, the 40 years of wandering, then, not only marks the beginning of a time when we were bodily free to observe Shabbat, but signifies as well the psychological

109

transition between being fully conditioned to accept forced labor, and being able to understand the rest and freedom encompassed in the *menucha* (מנוחה) or tranquility of Shabbat.

After life, Shabbat is the greatest gift God gave to man. It is said that the moment on Shabbat when everyone on earth rests from work, troubles and wars, the Messiah will come.

~ Rabbinic saying

There's more. Shabbat, like many of the Jewish holidays, is rooted in the ecology and physical characteristics of ancient Israel. We see this relationship manifested — if we realize what we're looking at — in the three symbols traditionally displayed on the Sabbath evening table: challah, wine and lights. The first is of course made from wheat, the second from grapes, and the third, originally from pure olive oil. Together they represent the three major crops of ancient Israel. They are especially difficult to grow, for all three (wheat, grapes, and olives) are dependent upon a delicate balance of sun, wind, and rain. Unlike their neighbors, the Hebrews depended on only one God to provide them with the vital combination. And, as appreciation of God's benevolence was demonstrated at the time by the sacrifice of produce, these three products became especially important Shabbat offerings in the Temple in Jerusalem. When the Temple was destroyed, one's home came to substitute as the synagogue, and one's table, the altar. Thus the Jewish people throughout their dispersion have so symbolized — sometimes unaware of the significance of the act — the deep bond which has always existed between themselves, their land, and their God. Each week they would symbolically sacrifice from the crops that were grown when the Jews were home on their soil.

As the Sabbath is beautifully ushered out with the *Havdalah* (הבדלה) service, we are reminded of one more connection between the Jews and their land. The wine and candles as symbols are somewhat explained above, but the spice box in this ceremony is an addition. Often called *hadass* (הדס), this term for the spice box translates literally into English as "myrtle," a plant also indigenous to Israel which releases a beautiful fragrance in strong sunlight. It is another symbol then of light and sweetness that helps the Jew to remember home.

With everything else that Shabbat offers us, it provides us as well with an opportunity to understand and appreciate our roots — in a very literal sense — for it allows us a glimpse into the lives, concerns, and prayers of our forefathers as they lived on — and off — the land.

──────────── .

Here are the minimal blessings to be made over the Shabbat symbols mentioned above as part of the Friday night ritual. But don't let these excerpts become an excuse not to get a complete prayerbook of your own!

upon lighting the candles:

Blessed are *You* Lord God,
King of the world, who has
made us holy with the deeds
You have required of us,
and who has obligated us to
light the light of Shabbat.

ברוך אתה ה׳
אלוהנו מלך העולם
אשר קדשנו במצותיו וצונו
להדליק נר של שבת.

before sipping the wine:

Blessed are *You* Lord God,
King of the world, who creates
the fruit of the vine.

ברוך אתה ה׳
אלוהנו מלך העולם
בורא פרי הגפן.

before eating the challah or meal:

Blessed are *You* Lord God,
King of the world, who takes
out bread from the earth.

ברוך אתה ה׳
אלוהנו מלך העולם
המוציא לחם מן הארץ.

מנוחה
Menucha

One

Not so long ago, to be Jewish was synonymous with being religious. One Shabbat, in a little Moroccan village, Saadia was on his way home from synagogue when he spotted Rahamim, a fellow Jew, standing on a corner openly smoking a cigarette. "Rahamim," gasped Saadia, "have you forgotten that it is Shabbat? "

"No," said Rahamim calmly, "I haven't forgotten."

"Rahamim," reproached Saadia, "have you forgotten, then, that smoking is prohibited on Shabbat? "

"No," said Rahamim undisturbed, "I am perfectly aware of that."

"Rahamim," sympathized Saadia, "you poor thing. Then you must have some strange disease, and the doctor has ordered you to smoke for health reasons."

"No," smiled Rahamim, "My body is in excellent shape." Saadia pondered for a moment. Having given Rahamim every benefit of the doubt, and every chance to explain away his sin, he finally turned his head upwards towards the heavens and exclaimed:

"God, what a people you have created! They may defile your day of rest, but never, never do they lie."

— Based on a traditional Jewish folktale

Two

"Rest in the sense of the traditional Sabbath concept is quite different from "rest" being defined as not working, or not making an effort (just as peace — shalom — in the prophetic tradition is more than merely the absence of war; it expresses harmony, wholeness.)

On the Sabbath, man ceases completely to be an animal whose main occupation is to fight for survival and to sustain his biological life. On the Sabbath man is full man, with no other task than to be human."

— Erich Fromm

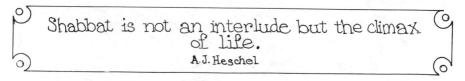

Shabbat is not an interlude but the climax of life.

A.J. Heschel

Three

"Six days a week we wrestle with the world, wringing profit from the earth; on the Sabbath we especially care for the seed of eternity planted in the soul. The world has our hands, but our soul belongs to Someone Else. Six days a week we seek to dominate the world, on the seventh day we try to dominate the self."

— A.J. Heschel

your turn Keep an account here of the ways you spend Shabbat in Israel. What do you do here, and how does that compare to what you did where you come from? What are your feelings about the day, about buses running or not running, about things being closed? Have a favorite place on Shabbat? A special something you like to do?

ALSO Go to town on a Friday afternoon and watch what happens as Shabbat approaches. What's being sold on almost every corner? Buy some and bring them back for the people you'll be with for Shabbat, even if that's only you.

Try to visit different synagogues on Shabbat. From tiny *shteibels* to new Reform temples, talk to the people and listen to their stories. You may not understand them and they might not understand you. But talk anyway; that's what it's all about.

נגונים
Niggunim

Niggun literally means "tune" in Hebrew. But a *niggun* is not just music because it has a soul as well. When you sing a *niggun* you can use the words that come with it, or else just make up some noises like "dai d'di dai" or "la la la." What matters is that you get so involved with the soul of the *niggun* that your own prayers and thoughts are contained within it. You have to try hard at first sometimes, but after a while it sort of just happens automatically.

On the next few pages are a few of our favorite *niggunim*. If you don't know their tunes, and no one around you does either, then you'll just have to make up your own: just sit back and relax, let your mind run free, close your eyes, sway a little, and sing. As the Baal Shem Tov taught us, *"Before you can find God, you must lose yourself."* If you're looking around for a time to try it, we recommend Shabbat services and meals. *Niggunim* are about the best thing we know of for helping to create Shabbat *ruach* (רוח)   — that full-of-peace spirit of Sabbath.

> The soul thou hast given me is pure.
> ~Siddur

> Song opens a window to the secret places of the soul.
> Hassidic saying

Oseh shalom bim'romav
Hu ya'aseh shalom alenu
V'al kal Yisrael, v'imru, – imru, amen
Ya'aseh shalom (2)
Shalom alenu v'al kal Yisrael

עושה שלום במרומיו,
הוא יעשה שלום עלינו
ועל כל ישראל ואמרו אמן.

He who makes peace up there
may He also make peace in the world of
down here, for us
And for all of Israel, and let us say, amen
He will make peace,
Peace for us and for all Israel

Esah eynai el he'harim
Mey-ayin, mey-ayin yavo ezri
Ezri me-et Ha-Shem
Oseh shamayim va-aretz

אשא עיני אל ההרים
מאין, מאין יבוא עזרי
עזרי מאת ה'
עושה שמים וארץ

I lift up my eyes unto the mountains
From where, from where will my help come
My help will come from the Lord
Maker of Heaven and Earth

אחת שאלתי מאת ה' אותה אבקש
שבתי בבית ה' כל ימי חיי
לחזות בנעם ה' ולבקר בהיכלו.

Achat sha-alti me-et Ha-Shem
Otah avakesh
Shivti b'vet Ha-Shem kal y'mey khaiyai
Lakhzot b'no-am, b'no-am Ha-Shem
Ul'vaker b'heykhalo

Only one thing I ask of the Lord
only one thing I seek
To dwell in the house of the Lord all the
days of my life
To savor the sweetness of God
and to behold His Temple

Ki miTziyon teytzey Torah
U'dvar Adonai m'Yerushalyim

כי מציון תצא תורה
ודבר ה' מירושלים.

(From Zion will go forth the Torah
and the word of God from Jerusalem)

Eli atah v'odekha
Elohai arom'mekha

אלי אתה ואודך
אלהי ארוממך.

You are my God and I thank You (for being there)
My God, I praise You.

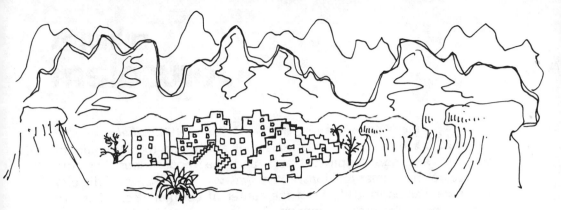

Section 6
URBAN RENEWAL

ירושלים
Jerusalem

think *"Yerushalayim shel mala"* and *"Yerushalayim shel matta,"* the Jerusalem of above and the Jerusalem of ·below. The ancient spiritual aura and the modern bustling city. Sacred to three great religions, *"Yerushalayim — Ir Shalom,"* the city of peace, has continually been the center of conflict. Yet it has also forever been the embodiment of the Jew's greatest hopes and profoundest dreams.

read What's the first thing that comes to mind when you think of:

Rehov Yafo

Hebrew University

Israel Museum

Maskit

Hadassah Hospital

Richie's Pizza

The Knesset

The Old City

Mt. Scopus

The Central Bus Station

Yad Vashem

Baltinester's

Mt. Herzl

The Holyland Hotel

118

The Jerusalem Hilton

King George Street

Jerusalem is:

( ) a city like any other
( ) a nice place to visit, but I wouldn't want to live there
( ) everything I'd expected
( ) the greatest city in the world

Note: This question, unlike the others in the book, has a correct answer. We don't want to give it away completely, but we'll give you a hint: it's not among the first three choices.

And now, your own thoughts:

ALSO get a hold of a copy of *Footloose in Jerusalem* by Sarah Fox (published by the Center for Jewish Education in the Diaspora of Hebrew University) and set out with some friends to explore.

connect

"In Jerusalem there are houses, sewage, buses, lampposts. Yet she is more than a city among cities; she is a city full of vision, a city with an extrasensory dimension. Her fascination is not in her age. She is a dwelling place, not a collection of monuments, shrines . . . Jerusalem is more than a place in space or a memorial of glories of the past. Jerusalem is a prelude, anticipation of days to come."

— A.J. Heschel

Jewish legend explains that the earth, as a creation of God, was formed similarly to the way in which a child develops inside its mother's womb. Beginning with the navel, the fetus evolves slowly into its finished shape. So too, the earth: from its central point, it grew into the globe we now live on.

And the navel of the world is Jerusalem.

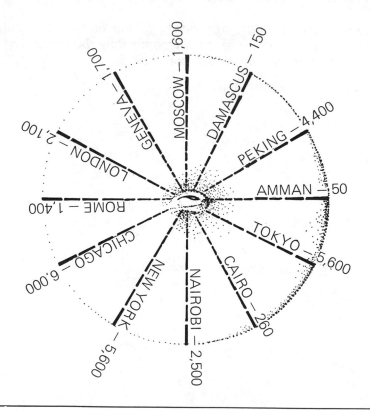

Jerusalem is the bellybutton of the world

know

Through history —
Egyptian texts from 19th-18th centuries BCE refer to "Rushalim" in first known reference to the city.

In his day, Abraham is welcomed to Jerusalem (known as "Salem") by King Melchizedek (Gen. 14:18).

Israelites enter Canaan in 13th century BCE; Jebusites control Jerusalem, known as Jebus.

King David conquers Jerusalem in 1000 BCE and names it City of David, declaring it his capital (II Samuel 5:6ff; I Chronicles 11:14ff).

King Solomon, son of David, builds First Temple in 10th century BCE, establishing Jerusalem as the spiritual and religious, as well as political, center of the ancient Hebrews.

Nebuchadnezzar, King of Babylonia, destroys Jerusalem and First Temple in 586 BCE.

Jews return from Babylonian Exile in 538 BCE and Jerusalem is restored by 455 BCE under Nechemiah.

Greeks capture Jerusalem in 320 BCE; in 165 BCE Maccabees regain and restore the city, making it the capital of the Hasmonean Dynasty.

Herod the Great, under Roman authorization, comes to rule the city in 37 BCE and builds elaborately in it.

Jerusalem and Second Temple destroyed by Romans in 70 CE and it becomes a Roman town.

In 636 CE Arabs capture Jerusalem, and for 500 years it becomes a Moslem center within which hundreds of mosques are built.

Crusaders seize Jerusalem in 1099.

Turks capture Jerusalem in 1517; in 1538 the Sultan Suleiman protects Jerusalem by building a wall around the city which still stands today.

In 1860 Sir Moses Montefiore creates first Jewish suburb outside the wall of the Old City.

British occupy Jerusalem in 1917 and maintain the seat of their Mandate government in it.

In 1948, with the Declaration of Independence, Jerusalem again becomes a Jewish capital. During the War of Liberation Jerusalem's 80,000 citizens are cut off from the rest of the State; holding out for a long period, they are finally able to retain only the new city.

For 20 years the city is artificially divided and Jewish holy places inside the walls of the Old City are desecrated

2000 BCE
1500
1000
500
BCE
0
CE
500
1000
1500
1800
1900
1925
1950

and destroyed under Jordanian rule.

During the Six Day War in June 1967 the city of Jerusalem is reunited under Jewish rule for the first time in 1,897 years.

1975

In 1977, Jerusalem has a population of some 300,000 people, of whom some 210,000 are Jews; the Knesset, Yad Vashem, Hebrew University, the National Library, the Israel Museum, and Hadassah Hospital are only a few of the many prestigious and world-renowned institutions within its limits.

2000

Dear Jerusalem

Legend may claim that you are the center of the universe, but to us you are the center of a problem.

Jerusalem, who can come to know you and doubt the messianic vision and the prophetic obligation of Israel to rise in its spiritual and moral capacities right up into the heavens? It is from you, so we are told — so we can feel — that *"will go forth the word of the Lord"* in leading the world to salvation in the end of days. As Jewish chauvinists who recognize our emotional investments, we find it hard to disagree with this concept of Israel as a "light unto the nations;" but how much of it can we accept as "political intellectuals," trying to be honest to our universalism?

On the one hand we feel obligated to work for your normalization — removing the stigma of chosenness and developing a nation that will not be subjected to castigation for falling prey to those problems which affect all other states. But at the same time, if we are to dedicate our lives to the building of a society and the preservation of a people, then it only makes sense that we be striving towards an idealism within that community, towards the evolution of a nation able to adopt a position of spiritual leadership in the world.

Jerusalem, you who are the heartbeat of Israel must help us. For what has your pulse been beating these thousands of years? To what end?

Here we are in your center and we still don't understand. We see your segregation by neighborhoods, the discrimination between your Jews of varied backgrounds, your unkempt and undisciplined children, your buses becoming pushier and pushier, the ugly buildings hiding your beautiful hillsides, the tensions between the Arab and Jewish segments of your population, and on and on.

But still we maintain our vision of the spiritual you; we have a memory of our people which in fact is probably not a memory at all but only a wishful fantasy; we have a knowledge of our history which might indeed be more dream than reality; and we have a concept, based purely on faith and not on a realistic assessment of any objective situation, of future Israel and of future *Am Yisrael*. So we can relate to you, Jerusalem, as more than just a reality; we can relate to you as well as a concept. We love both your sides; but then what choice do we have? In aiming towards what might be, our target must be sighted in the context of what is already here.

Jerusalem — a microcosm of Israel both in your beauty and your harshness. We roam along your streets, mingle with those who dwell in your midst, caress the stones of your most precious Wall, inhale your varied scents — your very breathing whispers in our ears.

Jerusalem, we stand witness to your accomplishments and we know deep inside of ourselves that you are both our challenge and our promise.

A Song

YERUSHALAYIM SHEL ZAHAV

ירושלים של זהב

Avir harim tsalul kayayin
Vereach oranim
Nisa beruach ha'arbayim
Im kol pa'amonim

אויר הרים צלול כיין
וריח ארנים
נשא ברוח הערבים
עם קול פעמונים.

Uv'tardeimat ilan va'even
Shvuya bachaloma
Ha'ir asher badad yoshevet
Uv'liba choma.

ובתרדמת אילן ואבן
שבויה בחלומה
העיר אשר בדד יושבת
ובלבה חומה.

Chorus:
Yerushalayim shel zahav
Veshel nechoshet veshel or
Halo lechol shirayich ani kinor.

ירושלים של זהב
ושל נחושת ושל אור
הלא לכל שיריך אני כנור.

JERUSALEM OF GOLD

Mountain air as clear as wine and the scent of pine, borne on the evening
wind with the sound of bells.
And in the slumber of trees and stone, imprisoned in her dream is the city
which dwells alone, a wall within her heart.

Chorus : Jerusalem of gold, of copper and of light,
Behold I am a harp for all your songs.

Naomi Shemer
©by the author

Jerusalem

Reality . . . and dream . . .

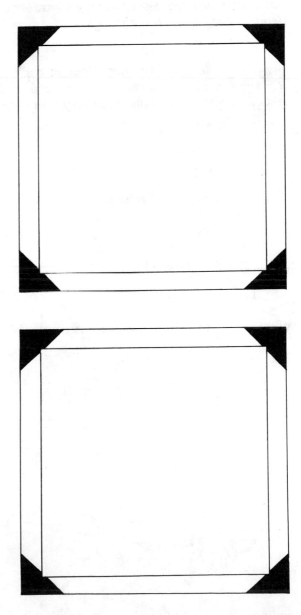

באר שבע
Be'ersheva

think Be'ersheva stands today as a gateway to the desert. Above it the countryside turns noticeably greener, but southward the desert sits as a silent challenge that few beside the *Bedouin* have been willing to dare.

react Instructions. Next to each word in Column B, place the number of the word in Column A that you most associate with it. Consider each response carefully.

Column A

1. Be'ersheva
2. Camels
3. The Negev
4. Wells of the Patriarchs
5. Desert
6. *Bedouin*
7. Israel south of Jerusalem
8. Making the desert bloom
9. Sand
10. Hot and dry

Column B

( ) desert
( ) desert
( ) desert
( ) desert
( ) desert
( ) desert
( ) desert
( ) desert
( ) desert
( ) desert

What else about the place, seriously now. (And don't say "desert"!)

126

connect One of David Ben-Gurion's life-long goals was the development of Israel's barren wastelands. He once exhorted a gathering of Zionist youth leaders:

"The deserts of Israel were once inhabited in ancient times and, even today, they are not entirely unpopulated. A beginning towards reclamation should be made by Jewish desert dwellers, Bedouins who will . . . find a way of making the desert into a place of settled habitation."

Ben-Gurion's vision is embodied by Be'ersheva's two part emblem: the first part is a tamarisk tree, symbolic of the ancient Hebrew's presence in the Negev, for as it says, *"Abraham planted a tamarisk-tree in Be'ersheva"* (Genesis 21:33). The second is a water pipe, a symbol of the revival of the Negev today.

know Be'ersheva is today the capital of Israel's southern district with an almost all Jewish population of some 81,000 people originating from all over the world. It was of great importance to each of the patriarchs because of the wells (*be'er,* באר — hence the city's name) which they either found or dug there, and later on it became the southernmost city of the Kingdom of Judah.

It was an Arab town in more recent times, until the War of Independence, during which time, after being a stronghold of the Egyptian army, it was captured by Israel in 1948. It has since become a center for cultural activity for southern Israel, now hosting Israel's newest university, appropriately named the Ben-Gurion University of the Negev.

Be'ersheva

Capital of the south . . . on the edge of the desert . . .

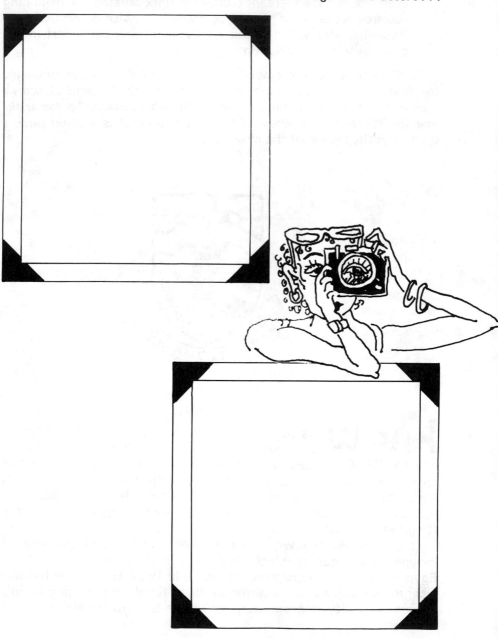

צפת
Tsefat

think A sacred city in Jewish tradition, Tsefat (also known as Safed) is the home of the *Kabbalah* — Judaism's unique treasure of religious mysticism. Numerous tiny synagogues, each with its own special story, are hidden in its alleyways.

But today the town is also the home of a picturesque artists' colony, as well as being one of Israel's favorite hide-away spots. Did the fine air, which today helps attract so many tourists, also have an influence on the Kabbalists who lived there almost half a millenium ago?

Mystical experiences I had in Tsefat:

Things I bought in Tsefat:

Places I visited in Tsefat:

Things I learned about in Tsefat:

Things I felt in Tsefat:

connect In the holy city of Tsefat lived a very poor man, but being a saint, he shared his meagre food with those who were even poorer than he.

As the Passover holiday came near, this meek saint fell gravely ill, and was no longer able to earn enough for even a crust of bread. His wife and children now went hungry. There seemed to be no chance at all that they would have enough money even to buy *matzah* and wine.

No one in Tsefat knew of the holy man's trials except Rabbi Isaac Luria, "The Holy Lion," the Master of the secret wisdom of the *Kabbalah*. He took off his white garments of sanctity and put on a wayfarer's dusty clothes. With a wanderer's staff in hand and a knapsack on his back, he went forth to aid the hidden saint.

For a while he passed to and fro before the poor man's house. Finally when the good man came out, he saw standing before him a dusty traveller.

"I've nothing to give you, but if you need a place for the holiday, you're welcome to stay with me," offered the saint.

The "traveller" was grateful and rejoiced in his good fortune. "Here are a hundred coins," he said to the poor man. "Prepare the Passover feast!"

On the first night of Passover the saint sat down to the *Seder*, but he would not begin without the stranger who had not yet returned from synagogue. But he waited in vain, for the stranger seemed to have disappeared. Suddenly it became clear to the poor man in a revelation. The stranger had been an angel sent by God to help him in his time of need! Yet neither he nor anyone else knew that the stranger was none other than the Holy Lion, the *Ari* himself.

— Based on a traditional Jewish folktale

know Rabbi Isaac Luria (better known by the acrostic *"ARI"*) lived in Tsefat during the 16th century. He was a major contributor — both in thought and practice — to the *Kabbalah*, the body of knowledge and philosophy that has come down to us as Jewish mysticism, said to be so powerful in its influence that a person is not permitted to begin learning it until the age of 40! In fact, the *Kabbalah* comprises a way of life emphasizing the spiritual element of existence, searching carefully into every crevice of the physical world in order to find the hidden bridges to God. Rules of logic and rationality are irrelevant to the stories and legends of the ways in which these Jewish mystics became drunk with Godliness.

It is the aura of this tradition which has settled over Tsefat, the capital of upper Galilee, and both the highest and northernmost large town in Israel. The Kabbalists made it the center of their learning in the 1500's, and there, in 1578, they used the first printing press in all of *Eretz Yisrael* and Asia. (It is still on display today.)

In recent centuries, not only the natural phenomenon of earthquakes, but also problems with inimical Druze and Arabs have made life for the Jewish population there difficult from time to time. Following a miraculous capture of the town (some 120 Jewish soldiers against 4000 Arabs) in the War of Liberation, however, the town has prospered and expanded. The Israeli government has recently announced plans to transform this town — with its own very down-to-earth urban problems — into a major city, aiming for some 200,000 people in the area by the 1980s.

Tsefat

A town of synagogues . . . and artists . . .

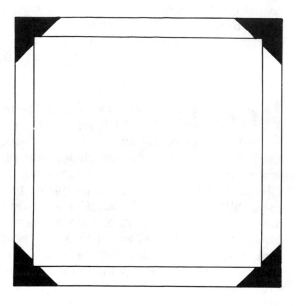

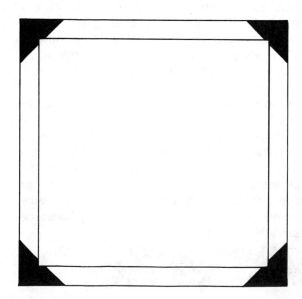

חיפה
Haifa

think The gold dome of the Bahai Temple, the smoke billowing from the cement-producing factories, the Egged buses running on Shabbat, and the deep blue Mediterranean viewed from the lush green of its mountain side are only a few of Haifa's distinguishing characteristics. Built on the slopes of Israel's famous Carmel mountain range, the city reminds many of America's San Francisco. And though the same basic ingredients went into it as into the rest of modern day Israel, this city is certainly unique unto itself.

read Things to do, visit, find out about, comment on, or research while in Haifa:

pollution/ Shabbat buses/ Mt. Carmel/ Bahai Temple/ *Carmelit*/ cement works/ shipping/ Technion/ illegal immigration/ Genesis 49:13/ Panorama/ Dan Carmel/ *Hadar*/ Haifa University/ three levels/ *Dagon*/ Maritime Museum/ Museum of Antiquities

connect A Zionist flag sewn together by hand from some old clothing and a banner proclaiming the ship *"Exodus from Europe — 1947"* were unfurled just as the boat chugged out of France's territorial waters.

A virtual floating sardine can, the ship — full to overflowing with Europe's displaced Jews who wanted desperately to get to Palestine — spent a week hobbling across the Mediterranean, shadowed relentlessly by British warships. As though the crew didn't have enough to worry about, food and water became immediately scarce, and the sanitation facilities quickly broke down. Closeted together in overcrowded and underventilated cabins, sickness took an especially high toll among the elderly. Nevertheless, the hundreds of destitute passengers tried to carry on as normally as possible — entertaining themselves, learning, discussing world politics, praying, dying in childbirth — even getting married.

And then suddenly one morning at 2 a.m., only 17 miles outside of Haifa, the ship received orders to halt and prepare to be boarded. When the captain, defying the instructions from the British (who were still officially in control of Palestine), quickly changed course, the *Exodus* was slammed from three sides. With its engines out and thus unable to move, there was nothing that could be done to prevent the British marines from jumping aboard. But once the soldiers were amongst them, the frenzied refugees struggled relentlessly against their would-be captors. Hot steam, boiling oil, teeth, bare hands, and whatever could be grabbed on to, were thrown into the battle. Fighting against the far more threatening small arms and tear gas, they were nevertheless able to hold out for six fierce hours.

When the Jews were finally overcome, six of their own lay dead and 120 wounded. Among the casualties were more than one young person whose parents had been murdered in Hitler's gas chambers.[6]

Such was the story of many "illegal" immigrant ships, part of *aliya bet* (עליה ב׳) , the immigration of refugees of Nazi Europe who courageously attempted to get to Palestine, in defiance of Britain's White Paper. Haifa's docks were as far as many of them got.

know Haifa is today Israel's third largest city with a population of some 220,000 people. Though mentioned in the Talmud in the third century CE, most of its history is obscure. Early in this century Haifa was overshadowed in importance by neighboring Acco, both as a port city and as a population center. With the advent of modern Zionism, it became a city in its own right, today claiming Israel's primary port, its heaviest industrial center, a major university, and a world renowned engineering institute (the Technion).

The root of Haifa's name is not known for certain, but those who say it is a contraction of the two Hebrew words *Hof Yafe* — beautiful coast — have a lot of supporting evidence in the city's physical setting!

Haifa

A city of beauty . . . and industry . . .

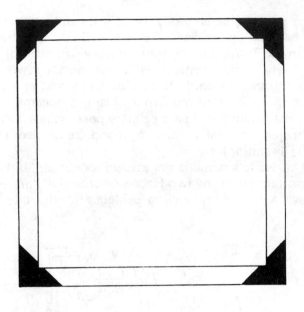

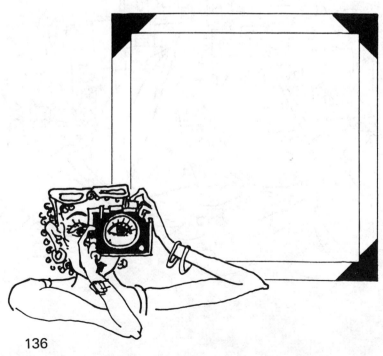

תל אביב
Tel Aviv

think In 1910, Tel Aviv was absolutely nothing but sand dunes. Today, the pizza parlors, tall buildings, discothèques, "houses of pleasure," and slums, hide even the ocean. Many people have a hard time deciding which they prefer.

read It's a real city! Not quite New York, I must admit, but it's not exactly the desert either. It's got everything: ....
....
Well, almost everything. After all, there are no ....
....
....
I think it's ....
.... that Israel has a place like this; if there were more...

When I think about it being all sand dunes only a few decades ago...

While in Tel Aviv, I...

137

connect The day David Ben-Gurion proclaimed Israel's Independence didn't end early for him; at 5 a.m. the next morning he was still busy in Tel Aviv, beginning a live broadcast to America.

Shortly after he started, however, he had to interrupt the address to inform his listeners that at the very moment Egyptian bombers were dropping their charges directly onto the city. As the crash of the explosions grew nearer and more fierce, he had to curtail the program altogether, as he could no longer even hear himself talk. He was later to recall:

> "Returning home, I saw the faces of all Tel Aviv peering through its windows; it was just sunrise. There was no hint of fear and panic, and I knew in my heart: they will stand up to it."

They did, helping to make true the Biblical prophecy that: *"Again I will build thee, and thou shalt be built"* (Jeremiah 31:3) It is inscribed on Tel Aviv-Jaffa's official emblem, a lighthouse over an open gateway, welcoming all into a restored Israel.

know Tel Aviv derives its name from the Hebrew translation of the title of Herzl's novel *Old-newland*. A *tel* is a hill composed of layers of ruins of ancient civilizations. *Aviv* means "spring." The implication is clear: on the very spot where it had once thrived, there was now to be a rejuvenation of Jewish life. The city was founded in 1909 and has developed at an amazingly fast rate. It serves as the center for business, entertainment, press, and publication in Israel today, and until 1948 was the first and only all Jewish, modern city. In 1949, contemporary Tel Aviv and ancient neighboring Jaffa merged and were renamed together Tel Aviv-Jaffa. The population of the city itself is over 300,000 while the greater metropolitan area holds 1,000,000 people — a full one third of Israel's total population!

Tel Aviv

A modern city . . . built on sand dunes . . .

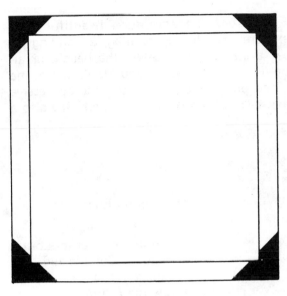

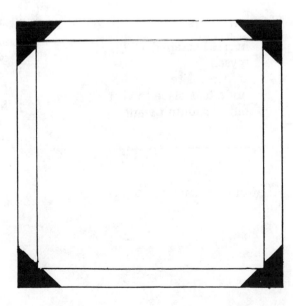

אילת

Eilat

think By day, Eilat offers the adventurer beautiful coral reefs to explore, and in the evening, depending on personal preference, either a star-lit *kumsitz* on the beach, or an action-packed discothèque in town. And if you don't mind the broken glass in the sand, the oil slick on the water, the oppressive heat in the air, and the hassle of *pushdakim* everywhere, it's also a great place for a swim!

react

Eilat is:

( ) beautiful
( ) dry
( ) paradise
( ) a city Israel
    could do without
( ) _____

The coral reefs:

( ) hurt! I scraped
    myself
( ) are exquisite
( ) not a bad place to visit,
    but I wouldn't want to
    live there
( ) _____

What did we leave out?

In and around Eilat I:

( ) visited the aquarium
    and underwater lookout
( ) swam to Coral Island
( ) finally got tan
( ) saw the *Fjörd*
( ) hiked through the
    canyon of the Inscriptions
( ) got badly sunburned
( ) slept on the beach
( ) snorkeled
( ) got bored
( ) found one place in Israel
    I wouldn't want to live
( ) found one place in Israel
    where I would want to
    live

140

connect

David Ben-Gurion repeatedly preached to his fellow pioneers:

"Now more than ever before we need a strong and devoted pioneering force. The desert area of our land is calling us, and the destruction of our people is crying out to us . . . The tasks that lie ahead will require great pioneering efforts the likes of which we have never known, for we must conquer and fructify the waste places . . . and we must prepare the way for new immigrants . . . First of all, we must conquer the sea and the desert, for these will provide us with room for new settlers and will serve as a laboratory for the development of new forms of economic and agricultural endeavor. We need men of the sea . . . who will make it a source of economic and political strength; we need men of the desert who will know it in all its secrets and will lead us in transforming the wasteland into a blessing, a place in which to work and live."

Eilat is but the beginning.

know

Eilat is as old as grafitti itself. In the surrounding mountains, a picture of a menorah was found carved into a rock wall. In this etching is inscribed (in Greek) a man's name, and the town from which he came, a Jewish community known to have flourished in Greek times. The *Eilah*, or terebinth tree, which grows in abundance in the area, gives the town its name.

In modern times, Eilat is one of the newest of Israel's cities, founded as late as 1950. It served first as a military base, but soon began to attract civilian settlers as a development town. Because of the location — Jordan, Saudi Arabia, and Israel all border on its gulf — Eilat is an area of great strategic importance. As Israel's only outlet to the Red Sea, it is an important harbor today even as it was in the time of the Kingdom of Judah. It has a population of only some 15,000 people, but also contains some of the fanciest hotels in the country. The Jordanian city of Aqaba faces it, and as both cities are expanding so rapidly, it is said that the two are having a night time "war of lights" across the gulf on which they both sit, within easy sight — and even swimming distance — of each other.

Eilat

Beaches . . . and beaches . . .

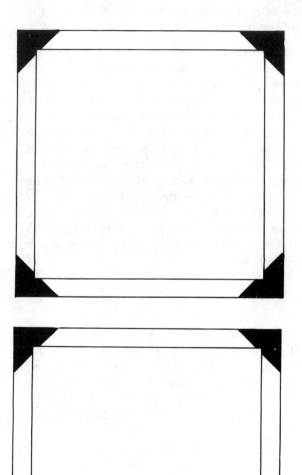

Section 7
DOMESTIC TSURIS

A Parable

A rabbi needed a new suit and went to a tailor in the village to have one made. The tailor promised it would be ready within a week, but when the learned man returned to pick it up, it was not yet finished. "Three more days," he was promised. Somewhat perturbed, but with no choice, the rabbi left the shop and came back again at the newly arranged time. Now the suit was indeed ready, and it fit perfectly — with not so much as a single stitch out of place. Impressed by the work but still annoyed about the delay, the rabbi scolded, "It should still have been done within the week."

"But rabbi," the tailor pleaded his case, "the suit I have created is flawless. Indeed God may have finished creating the world within a week, but just look at the state it's in!"

— Based on a traditional Jewish folktale

Give Israel some time. It too cannot be expected to be finished without mistakes "within the week." And as you read the next few pages, just remember that you're only trying to uncover the problems. Can you imagine what it's like for those who are trying to solve them?

Should Peace Break Out...

For the past few years, Israelis have been saying, "God forbid peace should break out." Of course peace is really the goal and the line is only said lightly, but nevertheless there's a very real concern expressed in it. That concern is that if there were not the threats of extinction coming from the Arab nations, Israel's social problems would erupt violently. The internal opposing factions would no longer feel any compulsion to present a common front, and the domestic bickering now going on would evolve into vehement battle.

This being a "write-it-yourself" book, it wouldn't be fair for us to go on writing endless pages of analysis of Israel's domestic troubles. But what we can do, since the subject is too important to ignore altogether, is to mention a few of the most controversial or significant points of a number of them, thereby providing you with a base for your own further exploration of the issues. Talk about them all with Israelis, *madrichim*, lecturers, friends, teachers, and tour guides; look out for news relating to them in the papers and on the radio; and in the spaces left blank, add to the confusion by writing about how you **personally** relate to it all. It's just too relevant to your being here to simply ignore.

(You might start exploring by finding out how the Israeli relates to problems in his or her society. If you see a protest or demonstration find out what it's all about. If you don't see one, find out what you can about any that have been held recently.)

The Social Gap

Perhaps the most disturbing of these problems is the tension which exists between Israel's Ashkenazi and Sephardi communities. The Ashkenazim are predominantly of European descent, and the Sephardim (or Oriental Jews) of Asian and African ancestry. The Ashkenazim were the first to "make *aliya*" with the emergence of political Zionism, and the Sephardim only began to come in large numbers within the last generation. The Ashkenazim were the founders of the majority of Israel's present institutions, and the Sephardim have been forced into adapting their lives to these established patterns. The Ashkenazim are the prime ideologues and movers of Israel's political parties, worker's union, educational system, and religious authority, while the Sephardim comprise some 60% of Israel's population.

FAMILY SIZE AND STANDARD OF LIVING

	origin of family:	
	Europe/America	Asia/Africa
average number of children per family (1968)	2.9	4.7
average monthly per capita income (1968)	385 I.L.	169 I.L.
per cent of families owning cars (1970)	19%	8%
per cent of families owning a TV (1970)	55%	48%

And if thy brother be waxen poor ...
then thou shall uphold him.
Leviticus 25:35

One specific phenomenon important to mention here is the "development town." Faced with the simultaneous needs following the War of Independence of settling strategic geographic regions and of absorbing masses of immigrants, Israel's leaders literally created

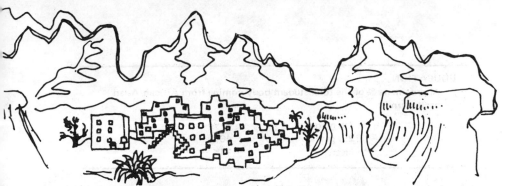

towns in the middle of nowhere. In some instances they took the potential settlers off the boats and brought them directly to the spots they needed populated — no questions asked. Many of these immigrants were Oriental. With little or no idea of what to expect in their new country, and without the know-how or relatives here to help them get what they wanted, many stayed where they were sent. Partly in consequence, some of these towns have remained without roots, have not received adequate governmental assistance, and are without vital educational, health, and social services. In short, they are generally problematic locales, often with vast numbers of what we term "culturally deprived" children. The authorities have made great efforts in recent years to alleviate the problems, but much is left to be done. Find out more if you can. What we've written here is only the briefest of accounts of the situation, and may prove misleading without further digging on your part.

% OF FAMILIES LIVING IN CROWDED CONDITIONS (3 or more persons per room)		
	1950	1971
ALL FAMILIES	21	8
BORN IN ASIA-AFRICA IMMIGRATED BEFORE 1947	37	12
IMMIGRATED SINCE 1947	49	17

Almost no one will argue that Israel's leaders acted intentionally to deprive the Sephardim of full participation in and benefit from the Israeli society, but certainly the State's founding fathers proceeded without the foresight and sensitivity that might have allowed for greater Sephardi input and gain all along. But the sharply distinct backgrounds of the two groups, the differences in their educational levels, the striking statistics on family size, and numerous other factors, make the existing discrepancies not only difficult to remedy, but understandably difficult to have avoided.

147

EDUCATION		
Approximate % of the total student body coming from African/Asian backgrounds:		
7th grade	61%	
12th grade	46%	
university	14%	

Meanwhile, we haven't yet discussed the specific problems that do exist between Ashkenazim and Sephardim. What are some of them? What are the cultural and religious differences? Do they have different aspirations? How are the two groups separated economically, occupationally, and educationally? Are there problems between the two groups regarding service in the Israel Defence Forces? What's the situation or effect of "intermarriage" between the two groups? What kind of social relations do exist? Are the groups physically divided by neighborhood, city, or region? What kind of political affiliation or representation does either group have? Who and what are the Israeli Black Panthers? When and why did they form? Do all Jews "belong" to one group or the other? Do any technically affiliate with either group? How has Russian immigration affected the existing problems? How has the Yom Kippur War?

your turn

ALSO Compare the rich and poor sections of the same cities. Are there slums? Walk into Nahlaut behind the Jerusalem *Hamashbir* department store and discover a whole different world.

דת
Religion

Contrary to the impression that many people in the Diaspora have, not everyone in Israel is religious. (Or haven't you noticed?) And the relations between those who are and those who aren't are oftentimes less than cordial. To some, simply being here is enough of an expression of their Jewishness. To others, being Jewish means having a cultural or national identity based in the Jewish past. And to only a minority — some 30% — does being a Jew mean strict adherence to Jewish law.

No problem, then, right? Each individual can choose his or her own way of life, and that's it. Wrong. Wrong, because since so much of Israeli life is by definition involved with being Jewish, everything from politics to education to public transportation is affected by such questions as: Who is a Jew? What is being Jewish? Who has the right to interpret the tradition? What is of public concern and what is a private matter? What should be transmitted to the next generation? And so on.

The questions which may have bored you in Hebrew schools outside Israel, have led to sometimes violent disputes here, where people have to live by the answers evolved. The problems don't accomodate "black and white" solutions, regardless of the side of the issue on which you stand:

Naturally anyone who wants to ride on a bus on Shabbat should be able to — unless you feel that there should be at least one place in the world where Shabbat is strictly observed.

Of course civil marriage is a part of contemporary civil liberties — but don't we have enough problems with assimilation in the Diaspora?

Certainly no one should be forced to study Jewish texts in school — unless, that is, Jewish texts are Israeli texts.

There is a deepening concern in Israel today that the young people growing up here identify themselves as Israelis and not as Jews, that they lack the ideological commitments of their parents to the ideals of a Jewish State, and that they feel estranged from other Jewish communities around the world. But it is recognized that this attitude is less apparent among the religious youth than among the secular.

How much tradition is the right amount of tradition? There are two parallel public school systems in Israel: one religious and one secular. Is widening the gap between the students compensated for by allowing everyone a greater freedom in choosing an atmosphere and course of study that he or she prefers? Or should the government decide just how much religion should be taught to everyone? What does separation of "church and state" really mean in *Eretz Yisrael*, where once religious law was also civil law?

your turn

חינוך
Education

Israelis go to school six days a week — as inconceivable as that might sound! It's compulsory until the age of 15, and free until either 9th or 10th grade (depending on where one lives). Though more is spent nationally on education than on anything else in Israel except defense and housing, the funds still just don't exist to extend tuition-free schooling through the 12th grade.

As long as the students do keep going, though, Israeli law says they're supposed to be getting an education based

> "on the values of Jewish culture and the achievements of science; on love of the homeland and devotion to the State of Israel and the Jewish people; on training in agricultural labor and handicrafts; on fulfillment of pioneering principles; on the aspiration to a society built on liberty, equality, tolerance, mutual aid, and love of fellow man."

Talk to young Israelis to find out about what really does go on in school from their point of view. Find out about youth movements, vocational high schools, *Gadna, Yeshivot*, seminaries, and universities. Also, for two of the more controversial issues of education, see the paragraphs in this section on religion and the social gap.

your turn

צבא
Army

In Israel, at 18 you go into the army. One doesn't have to worry about applying; there's almost no such thing as a rejection. As security needs change, so does the time of service, but at the moment men serve for three years initially, and then for up to 35 days a year in the reserves until they're 55. Women serve two years in the beginning, and then may be called up for reserves until they marry or become pregnant. Along with the economic problems of making a go of it here, emigrating Israelis often cite this tough military duty as a major reason for leaving. On the other hand, many Israelis living abroad will rush back to Israel and report to the army the moment any trouble breaks out.

How do you feel about the idea of serving in the Israel Defense Forces (צה"ל) ? What about the army where you come from? And in a country where every citizen learns how to fight, do you end up with a society of soldiers, or an army of civilians? How militaristic is Israel? And what effect does the security situation seem to have on everyday life here?

your turn

נשים
Women

This is a strange country. A woman can become Prime Minister, yet in most synagogues she isn't allowed to read from the Torah, and in some she's hidden away in the back where she can't even see who does. And whereas women once fought side by side with men in the War of Liberation, today their role in the army is generally that of secretary, clerk, teacher, or morale booster. Even on kibbutz, where equality is a guiding principle, the women generally content themselves with taking care of the children, running the kitchen, and washing the clothes, while the men work out in the fields or run the factories. How does the Israeli woman react to all of this? What are her goals in life? What jobs does she hold? How often is she pregnant? How does she feel men view her? And how does she want them to? What do the men feel about it all?

your turn

מדיניות
Politics

Israel's legal and political structure is made up of a little bit of this and a little bit of that: Talmudic, Turkish, British, and contemporary law have all been incorporated into the Jewish State's governmental system. Find out what you can about the executive, legislative, and judicial branches of the government. How are people elected? For what positions? For how much time? How representative are they? To what political parties do they belong? How many parties are there? What do they stand for? What is a coalition government?

your turn

הערבים שבפנים
The Arabs Within

There are almost half a million Arabs living in Israel proper today. The State has made a considerable effort to allow them full cultural, religious, and social autonomy, while simultaneously attempting to integrate them into the mainstream of Israeli society as much as possible.

Still many crucial problems remain, perhaps the most outstanding being for the individual himself: where do his loyalties lie? At least as long as there exists a state of war between Israel and her neighbors, this dilemma will continue. In the meantime, Arabs are exempted from military service — officially to relieve them from any conflict of conscience. Yet this in itself is a problem. Serving in the army in Israel today is a major part of integrating into mainstream society, and an important factor in coming to feel this country is yours.

From the point of view of the Israeli Jew, there is also a problem, and that is overcoming stereotypes and prejudice, understandably having resulted in part from having had to fight in so many unwanted wars, in which so many relatives and friends have been killed.

Finally, there is an ideological consideration. A primary purpose of Zionism has been to establish a framework in which the Jews would have an opportunity to create their own collective way of doing things. Surely the same needs must exist for the Arab communities. How can one government provide adequate direction, leadership, and resources for both developments — and are these developments even compatible within the same state? Can bi-nationalism work? (It was tried in Lebanon.) But what other alternatives are there?

What type of solution would permit the continuation of a Jewish State without making non-Jews feel left out? And here is the dilemma: On the one hand, we cannot be expected to give up our right to self-determination for the sake of another group; on the other hand, if the minority group members within our midst feel themselves to be second class citizens, then by definition we do not have a Jewish State based on Jewish values.

> And a stranger shall thou not oppress; for ye know the heart of a stranger, seeing ye were strangers in the land of Egypt.
>
> ~Exodus 23:9

your turn

The Arabs I've seen in Israel have been
....
....
Seeing them ....
with the Jews makes me feel ....
....
I wonder how they really feel about the country . . .

There's been a lot of unrest, I understand, and not only in the occupied territories, but among the indigenous population in Israel proper. Though their standard of living, level of health care, and educational opportunities are greater here in the Jewish State than in many places in the Arab world, apparently the violent disturbances . . .

I think Israel's policy towards them should be . . .

ALSO Find out what's on the mind of an Arab you're buying something from in the Old City of Jerusalem; approach an Arab on the West Bank; talk with an Arab student at some university.

עליה
Going Up?

Kibbutz hagaluyot (קבוץ הגלויות) means "ingathering of the exiles." It refers to the dream of bringing together — in *Eretz Yisrael* — Jews from all over the world. But each group that arrives comes from a different background — with a set of customs, values, educational goals and attitudes all its own. To keep us all together, the immigration authorities once sought to mix everybody up in a big Jewish melting pot; then it was discovered that people don't melt. Now the policy is cultural pluralism, and immigrants are encouraged to preserve their own distinguishing characteristics, while the Government simultaneously attempts to strengthen the bonds Israelis feel to the Jewish State and the Zionist ideals.

Still difficulties arise. It is sometimes said lightly that Israelis love *aliya* (עליה ← immigration), but could do without the *olim* (עולים ← immigrants)! Although the phrase is more cynical than is the reality, the truth hinted at here is that though veteran Israelis unanimously agree that more Jews must be brought into Israel, they often don't welcome them with open arms on a one to one basis. One of the reasons for this is that the newcomers receive generous stipends, large tax breaks, subsidized housing, and free professional training or

157

schooling from the government during their first few years here. This policy is explained as involving the least that can be done to help the new immigrant adapt to his or her new society. But it's hard for the Israeli who's been here for years building the country, paying outrageous taxes, living in cramped quarters, and serving long periods in the army, to see it that way — especially if the *oleh* (עולה) is wealthier than the *sabra* (צבר) to begin with.

On the other side of the coin, is the new immigrant who, in the same vein, will occasionally sigh, "We love Israel; it's just the Israelis we can't stand." Again an exaggeration, but again a morsel of truth. Often the *olim* will arrive here full of infatuation with both the land and concept of Israel. But they may be unaware that to the vast majority of oldtimers (ותיקים),   Israel is simply home, and not a Garden of Eden. The idealistic newcomers find it hard to accept that their adopted compatriots don't always share their excitement in being here. Furthermore, unprepared for the rigors of day to day life here, and used to established patterns of doing things "back home," they react with great indignation when confronted by the unfamiliar Israeli ways of getting things done — or leaving them unfinished!

158

your turn

The people in Israel, they're................
.... Different faces, clothes,
.... and .... I've met Israelis
from at least .... different countries, speaking .... languages.
Jews from so many different countries, all together it . . .

The whole idea of *aliya*, of people deciding to come and live here ......
....
The things that must make them decide to take the step . . .

Me personally, I feel ....
.... where I live. The idea of coming to Israel permanently . . .

ALSO Talk to someone a lot older and try to find out why he or she is here. When, why, and from where did the person or person's parents come? What does each think about living here?

Talk to Russian Jews at an absorption center (first find out what an absorption center is — hint, ask someone in immigration and not in water conservation) and discover what kind of problems they had back in Russia and how they were able to come on *aliya*.

Talk to an American Jew that has made *aliya*. What made him or her give up the life he or she had in the U.S. and move to Israel? Ask the person about "standard of living" and "quality of life."

Going Up?

Ingathering of the exiles...

ירידה
Yerida

There are presently some 750 Israeli taxi drivers in New York City. They're part of the more than 300,000 Israelis currently living in the United States. Being that there are barely 3,000,000 Jews in Israel to begin with, it means that more than one out of ten Israelis has left home. Put these numbers alongside the fact that more than half of the *olim* from free western countries eventually go back to where they came from, and that over 50% of the Russian Jews leaving the Soviet Union now don't even get to Israel in the first place, and you have a problem — or at least a long set of questions:

First of all, why are they leaving? The better economic and educational opportunities in America are not enough of an explanation. Every such move is caused by both a "push" and a "pull." What are the elements of Israeli society that discourage people from staying?

Secondly, what should be the attitude towards those who leave? Are Israelis any more obligated to stay in their homeland than are Jews abroad to make *aliya*? As one *yored* — emigrant (יורד) once said to us, defending her new life in America, "I put in my time in Israel; no one has to live there permanently, but every Jew has to give it a try." And then there's the sentiment often expressed that no matter how much money a Diaspora Jew contributes to the UJA, it doesn't compare to standing on the front lines in Israel. *Yordim* often think it's time to change places for a while.

Talk to people here about it all. Especially for those who are contemplating staying in Israel, it's important to know why others are leaving. It says something about the society: its day to day problems, the identity of those who make it up, and the relationship between it and Jewish communities around the world.

your turn

הסכסוך הערבי-הישראלי
The Israel-Arab Conflict

This is really an international, and not simply a domestic, problem. Yet the tragic state of belligerency that has always existed between Israel and her Arab neighbors has affected every single other aspect of Israeli society.

The Arab governments claim that an end to the conflict depends both on finding a solution to the Palestinian refugee problem, and on Israel's willingness to withdraw from all Arab occupied territory. Yet most Israelis claim that the Arab antagonism pre-dates even the existence of these issues, and that the real obstacle to peace is the on-going Arab refusal to acknowledge the Jews' very right to a state of their own. The arguments over the origin of the dispute are no less complicated.

But we cannot even begin to discuss the controversy here in any meaningful way. It's a topic you'll just have to explore on you own. (The two books by Walter Laquer under "Reading into it . . ." are excellent for this.) Try to uncover the conflicting claims to the same piece of land, the beginnings of the Jewish and Arab national liberation movements, the numerous positions the two sides have taken all along, the various options that have been put forward for bringing the conflict to a close, and the changing attitudes the international community has adopted towards the sides over the past 30 years. We leave it to you, then, to fill in the history of the changing boundaries drawn on the maps below. Just realize, however, that there have always been two sides to the conflict — right or wrong — and that to defend one, you must understand the other.

your turn

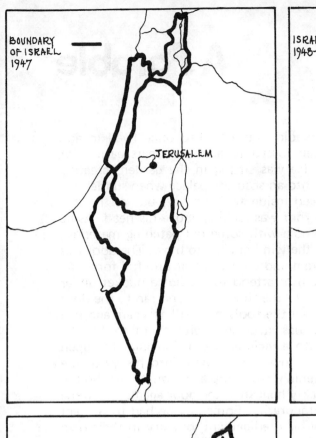

BOUNDARY
OF ISRAEL
1947

JERUSALEM

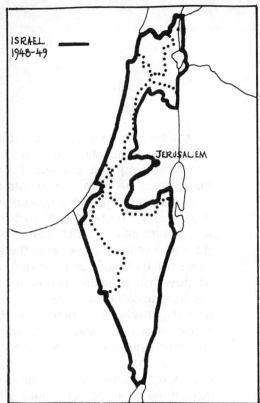

ISRAEL
1948-49

JERUSALEM

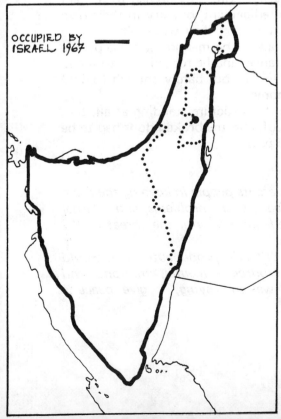

OCCUPIED BY
ISRAEL 1967

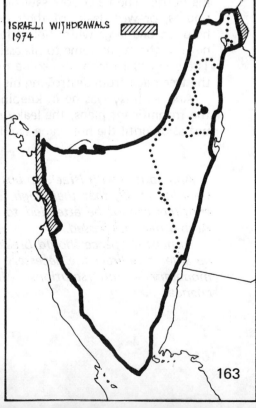

ISRAELI WITHDRAWALS
1974

163

A Parable

A man returned to a very old house he had once lived in and loved, but which he had been forced to abandon years earlier for reasons beyond his control. He was sitting in the garden, creating magnificent plans to turn it into an absolute palace when suddenly a slight drizzle began. He moved inside to keep dry, but as the rain increased, he found that the roof was leaking above his head. As he was attempting to block the hole with some old patching materials, the rain became heavier and the wind started to blow. The door was flung off its hinges and the rain and cold came at him full force. As he now had a greater problem to attend to, he put a bucket under the hole to catch the dripping for the time being, and ran to the door to put it back on its hinges. All the tools he had left years ago had rusted, however, and as he was struggling with them to fix the entrance, the rains turned into a vicious storm. Through the open door he noticed a tree leaning over menacingly into his yard, the impending hurricane threatening to topple it onto his house, destroying it altogether. Quickly he leaned the door against its frame and propped it into place temporarily. Somehow he had to protect his house. The neighbors saw his predicament, but dry in their own houses, or with leaks of their own to fix, they wouldn't come to help. In one large white house far away the man knew some people he thought might come to his assistance, and he rushed over to them. They agreed to loan him some materials, but barely enough to hold the tree back from destroying his home.

And so busy was he in keeping the structure standing at all, that the magnificent plans, the leaky roof, and the broken door had to be put aside until the hurricane would pass.

And so it is with Israel. So busy are its people in keeping the State standing at all, that their high ideals, social problems, and internal conflicts cannot be attended to adequately until the threat of the Arab armies has passed.

Perhaps if "peace should break out", the proper authorities would be able to redirect the necessary resources — mental, emotional, and monetary — into solutions. All we are saying, is give peace a chance . . .

Other problems? Want to know more about any of these? We recommend Amos Elon's **The Israelis: Founders and Sons** (listed in this book's "Reading into it" section). An excellent perspective that's good reading. Also, the Youth and Hechalutz department (listed under "Looking for something?") will be glad to provide you with up-to-date material it produces on varied dimensions of Israeli society, as will the Israel Information Center (in the same list).

A Song

LU Y'HEE

לו יהי

Od yeish mifras lavan b'ofek
עוד יש מפרש לבן באופק

Mul anan shachor kaved
מול ענן שחור כבד

Kol sh'n'vakeish lu y'hee
כל שנבקש לו יהי

V'im b'chalonot ha'erev
ואם בחלונות הערב

Or neirot hachag roed
אור נרות החג רועד

Kol sh'n'vakeish lu y'hee.
כל שנבקש לו יהי

Chorus: Lu y'hee
לו יהי

Lu y'hee
לו יהי

Ana lu y'hee
אנא לו יהי

Kol sh'n'vakeish lu y'hee.
כל שנבקש לו יהי

Ma kol anot ani shomeia
מה קול ענות אני שומע

Kol shofar v'kol tupim
קול שופר וקול תופים

Kol sh'n'vakeish lu y'hee
כל שנבקש לו יהי

Lu tishma b'toch kol eila
לו תשמע בתוך כל אלה

Gam t'fila achat mipee
גם תפילה אחת מפי

Kol sh'n'vakeish lu y'hee.
כל שנבקש לו יהי

Chorus: Lu y'hee. . .
לו יהי . . .

B'tosh sh'chuna k'tana mutselet
בתוך שכונה קטנה מוצלת

Bai'it kat im gag adom
בית קט עם גג אדום

Kol sh'n'vakeish lu y'hee
כל שנבקש לו יהי

B'sof hakai'its, b'sof haderech
בסוף הקיץ, בסוף הדרך

Ten l'hem lashuv halom
תן להם לשוב הלום

Kol sh'n'vakeish lu y'hee.
כל שנבקש לו יהי

Chorus: Lu y'hee. . .
לו יהי . . .

V'im pitom tizrach m'ofel
ואם פתאום תזרח מאופל

Al rosheinu or kochav
על ראשינו אור כוכב

Kol sh'n'vakeish lu y'hee
כל שנבקש לו יהי

Az ten shalva v'ten gam coach
אז תן שלוה ותן גם כוח

L'kol eile sh'nohav
לכל אלה שנאהב

Kol sh'n'vakeish lu y'hee.
כל שנבקש לו יהי

Chorus: Lu y'hee. . .
לו יהי . . .

Still the white sail in the distance
Facing black and heavy cloud
All that we shall ask, let it be
And through the windows of the evening
Flicker festive lights so proud
All that we shall ask, let it be.

Chorus : Let it be
Let it be
O please let it be
All that we shall ask, let it be.

What answering calls do I hear,
Voice of *shofar* and of drum
All that we shall ask, let it be
May you hear among them
A prayer also from me
All that we shall ask, let it be.

In the small and shadowed neighborhood
Is a small house, red-roofed its look
All that we shall ask, let it be
At summer's end, the end of the way
Let them return to this nook
All that we shall ask, let it be.

If, suddenly, will shine from the darkness
On our heads the light of a star
All that we shall ask, let it be
Then, but give peace and also give strength:
To all our loved ones, near and far
All that we shall ask, *Let it be.*

—Naomi Shemer
© by the Author

Section 8

PUTTING IT ALL TOGETHER

Snap Reactions

When we stop writing, you keep going... Put down the first thing that comes to your mind, and then figure out how it got there.

1. When I see Jerusalem from a distance I feel ...

2. When I see old Jews at the Wall I feel ...

3. When I see young Jews at the Wall I feel ...

4. When I see Jews fighting with each other I feel ...

5. When I see a bus driver with a *keepah* I feel ...

6. When I see a Jewish beggar I feel ...

7. When I see "pushdakim" I feel . . .

8. When I see Israelis pushing to get onto buses I feel . . .

9. When I see tall modern apartment houses in Jerusalem I feel . . .

10. When I see a "real" city like Tel Aviv I feel . . .

11. When I see theatres and museums here I feel . . .

12. When I see a hand-planted forest in Israel I feel . . .

13. When I see how barren the Negev is I feel . . .

14. When I see an Israeli soldier I feel . . .

15. When I see the Arab borders I feel . . .

16. When I see things of war (a fighter plane overhead, an army base, an explosion in the distance) I feel . . .

17. When I see an Arab refugee camp I feel . . .

18. When I see people laughing, crying, talking, yelling, and loving in Hebrew, I feel . . .

19. When I see me here I feel . . .

You're On Your Own

*Money is hard to come by in Israel. Very hard. As a tourist you may not have to worry about it too much. But you should know what the Israelis are up against. Ask them; they'll be glad to tell you. It's one of their favorite topics of conversation.

But relatively speaking, traveling around is still reasonable, safe, and easy. Transportation, accomodations, and food are everywhere accessible and everywhere affordable. But there are a few things you should know before you take off.

Transportation

1. An Egged bus is a very strange animal.

2. An Egged bus driver is a very strange animal.

3. Egged bus drivers generally own their Egged buses. Egged buses run the country. They have a monopoly most places. They are indispensible. The drivers know this and they let you know that they know it. They are also amongst the highest paid "professionals" in Israel. Sometimes if they don't like the way you're acting, they'll ask you to get off the bus. The bus won't move again until you do.

4. Egged buses live in central cages in each city and town, called the *takhana merkazit* (תחנה מרכזית), or central bus station. **Everyone** knows where it is and how to get there. If you want to find out too, go up to someone and say, *"Ey-foh ha-ta-kha-na ha-mer-ka-zit?"* (?איפה התחנה המרכזית) That means, "where is the central bus station?" if you say it correctly. They will probably tell you in English, or else say *"Yashar, yashar, v'yemina"* (ישר ישר וימינה) which means, "straight ahead and to the right," which is where everything in Israel seems to be located.

5. At the *takhana merkazit* there is a small information cage in which the bus-keeper sits and gives out information — usually correct, but not always. Sometimes tickets are sold there too. If not, he can tell you where they are.

6. Buses go to everywhere in Israel — not just to the cities and

---

We'll be giving certain equivalencies of Israeli lirot in U.S. Dollars. If you've got other currencies with you, you'll have to convert accordingly. Sorry we couldn't provide a pocket calculator with this book.

towns, but to all the kibbutzim and little villages too. In the cities they run very comprehensive and frequent routes.

7. Egged buses sleep on Shabbat, except for a few spunky ones, mostly in Haifa.

8. When Egged buses are sleeping, you can take a *sherut* (שירות) . A *sherut* is like a limousine and goes between cities and also within cities for only a little more than a bus. Taxis also never sleep, and you can take one almost anywhere, but for a lot more money. If you want to find the *sherut* station, go up to someone and ask, *"Ey-foh yesh she-rut?"* (?איפה יש שירות) You might think the plural of *sherut* is *sherutim*. You're right, except that the word literally means "service," and for some reason, "services" in Hebrew means toilet or bathroom. If you ask someone, *"Ey-foh ha-she-rut-im?"* (איפה ?השרותים) they'll tell you, but the directions won't get you from Tel Aviv to Jerusalem.

9. Bus rides are fairly cheap. But prices are constantly going up. In June, 1973, it cost 3.50 IL (Israeli Lirot), or just over $.80 to go from Jerusalem to Tel Aviv (about 63 kilometers, 38 miles, and an hour and a quarter.) In the spring of 1977 it cost about $1.50 for the same ride — and you didn't get there any faster. Inside the cities, the price for an average ride was 20 agorot just a few years ago, now it's 1.10 Israeli Lirot, but chances are it will stay way under a quarter for some time yet. Part of this rise in prices is caused, by the way, by the fact that gas now costs somewhere near to $2.50 a gallon.

10. Special bus passes that give you unlimited travel within a certain time period are available at a big savings. If you're planning on doing a lot of traveling, it might be worthwhile getting one. You can check out details at a *takhana merkazit*, an office of Egged Tours, or at one of the Israel Government Tourist Offices (listed under "Looking for something? ")

11. Hitch-hiking is generally very safe, but not very successful. Soldiers will always get rides before you. If you're in a rush, forget about it. If you've got a lot of time, it might be worth trying. It's one way to meet Israelis. But with the risk of sounding sexist, we should add that females should be wary of overly "friendly" males, especially if hitching alone. By the way, hitching in Israel is called *tramping* — even in Hebrew. Also, you don't get rides the same way all over the world. Instructions for Israel: face the traffic, stretch out your right arm downwards towards the road, with your pointer (that's the finger next to your thumb) extended. Got it?

12. Nothing is very far away from anything else in Israel. Below is a chart of distances between some of the major cities. For traveling time by bus, you can estimate it taking somewhere around an hour of traveling time for every 50 kilometers — give or take a few flat tires.

DISTANCES		Kilometers*	Miles*
Jerusalem to	Haifa	151	94
	Tel Aviv	63	38
	Nablus	65	41
	Jericho	34	21
	Bethlehem	8	5
	Beersheba	86	54
Tel Aviv to	Haifa	95	59
	Beersheba	107	67
	Gaza	76	48
Beersheba to	Eilat	233	146

* 1 kilometer (km) – 62 miles; 1 mile = 1.61 km.; in any case, a kilometer is shorter than a mile.

Accomodations

1. Some 30 youth hostels have been constructed across Israel. They're cheap. They are not luxurious.

2. Israeli youth hostel administrators can be fairly strict about hostel membership cards. It you don't have one though, you can almost always come in as a guest with someone who does, but it will cost you a little more. If they're not crowded, you can also generally come in without a card or a member. If you want a card, you can get one in Israel at the office listed below. Prices keep changing, but it will probably cost you about $7.50 to $8.00.

3. Hostels cost around $3.00 a night, including breakfast. Check the latest Youth Hostels bulletin, though, for latest details, available free from their office, as is a list of all the hostels, and hostel rules and facilities. (Address under "Looking for something? ")

4. Prepared meals, except for breakfast, are not always available to individuals who are staying at hostels. When they are, a meat meal costs around $2.00, a dairy one, about $1.00. For those a little more adventurous, though, the hostel kitchen (with pots and pans but no eating utensils) is always available for your use for a minimal charge.

5. Hostels are good places to meet friendly young people from all over the world.

6. Hostels are good places to get ripped off by friendly young people from all over the world. The rooms sleep a lot more than one person, usually in bunk beds. Keep your stuff as safe as possible during the night.

7. Hostels are generally locked all day. Your stuff is pretty safe inside, but you won't be able to get to it until late in the afternoon if you leave it there in the morning. Remedy: take with you what you'll need for the day when you start out.

8. There are all sorts of hotels in Israel costing from as little as $4.00 or $5.00 a night. Those with the pools and the views and the carpets cost a lot more, and unless you have a good $40.00 or so to waste, we recommend a little free lobby-sitting as the way to find out what goes on inside them.

9. The beaches and parks are generally free, sometimes very companionable, but not always legal or safe for sleeping in. You'd better check out each one carefully before making any decisions.

Food

1. Food in Israel is mostly vegetables which are mostly not very expensive and mostly very good.

2. The corner grocery stores (the *makolet*--מכולת) are very common in Israel. Modern supermarkets are now springing up almost everywhere too, and open air markets can be found frequently.

3. Restaurants are everywhere, and felafel (פלפל) stands are everywhere everywhere.

4. Between restaurants, felafel, and vegetables you can manage on

$3.00 or at most $4.00 per day for food while traveling, very nicely for $5.00 a day.

5. Some of the cheapest food can be found at the university snack bars and cafeterias. Worth checking out in Jerusalem, Tel Aviv, Haifa, and Be'ersheva.

6. For non-vegetarians, *shwarma* (שוורמה) is definitely worth trying when you get tired of felafel. *Humus* (חומוס), *techina* (טחינה), and *salat chatzilim* (סלט חצילים) are favorite stand-bys, and also rather cheap in most smaller restaurants and cafes.

7. *Ice-cafe* is an Israeli specialty, and is delicious but a little extravagant in some places.

8. New York Jewish delicatessen cannot be found; don't bother looking. You'll have to manage with the imitation stuff which in a few places is now edible. (If you're not from New York, just as well that you don't know what you're missing.)

9. You can find kosher places everywhere. If they are legitimate (almost all are), then they'll have a *te'udah* (תעודה) or certificate, from the Rabbinate. You can ask to see it, and they'll be glad to show it to you — if they've got one.

10. You won't starve.

Miscellaneous

1. All in all, $15.00 per day while traveling is more than adequate. It's certainly possible on $10.00, and maybe even on $7.00, but that might get very tight. It depends on your appetite, how much touring you plan on doing, and the kind of luxury you demand. (None of this includes souvenirs, shopping, etc., by the way.) Package deals either with Egged, the Israel Youth Hostel Association, the Israel Student Travel Association, or the Israel Government Tourist Office can really help. (Addresses under "Looking for something?")

2. What to see, where to go, how to find it. Check out the Israel Government Tourist Offices. The people in them can really be very helpful, or at least give you a lot of very pretty and colorful brochures. (Addresses under "Looking for something?")

3. The Israel Student Tourist Association (ISSTA) runs all sorts of quickie tours, as well as some longer ones. They can also help with

information in general, especially about travel. (Offices listed under "Looking for something?")

4. Wherever you go, take a copy of a guide to Israel with you (available in any bookstore.)

5. Bring or get an international I.D. card (available in Israel from the Israel Student Travel Association.) It gets you all sorts of discounts, most notably on bus rides.

6. Carry travellers' checks, not cash. You can cash them everywhere (with your passport), and many places give a substantial discount on purchases made with them.

7. Office hours and store hours are crazy in Israel. Somewhere there must be an accurate and comprehensible listing. Generally, banks, post offices, and most stores are closed from around 1 p.m. – 4 p.m. (opening in the morning around 8:30 or 9:00 and closing in the evening around 7:00, except banks, which close around 5:00). Eating places do not generally close during that mid-day break. Other types of offices are usually open from around 9:00 – 3:00, though that changes with the season. Rule: check before you shlep.

8. This is what your money's worth** (average items)

cost in IL*	1970	1973	1977	197_
city bus	.25	.45	1.10	
soft drink	.50	.70	3.00	
pay phone	.20	.25	.50	
felafel	.70	1.20	4.00	
movie	2.00	4.00	13.50	
camel	1 sister	3 sisters	6 sisters	
good meal	4.00	7.00	35.00	
sandals	15.00	23.00	120.00	
aerogram	.50	.55	1.90	
waterpipe	12.00	15.00	80.00	
record	18.00	25.00	47.00	
$1.00**	3.50	4.20	9.00	

* IL = Israeli Lira = 100 agorot
** At the banks, that is.

Warning: It is said that the way to make a small fortune in Israel is to bring a large fortune with you.

Looking For Something?

ISRAEL GOVERNMENT TOURIST OFFICES

for all sorts of help in planning your stay and getting around

Jerusalem
24 Rehov Hamelekh George
Tel. (02) 227281/2
Jaffa Gate
Tel. (02) 282295/6

Tel Aviv
7 Rehov Mendele
Tel. (03) 223266/7

Haifa Town
Tel. (04) 666521
16 Rehov Herzl
Tel. (04) 666523

Haifa Port
Shed No. 12
Tel. (04) 663988
Shed No. 14
Tel. (04) 645692

Lod
Ben Gurion Airport
Tel. (03) 971485/7

Allenby Bridge

Akko (Acre)
Municipality Building
Tel. (04) 910251

Arad
Magen David Adom Building
Tel. (057) 97012/3

Ashqelon
Commercial Centre, Afridar
Tel. (051) 2739

Be'er Sheva
Bet Tnuat Hamoshavim
Tel. (057) 76011 — 73337

Bethlehem
Manger Square
Tel. (02) 942591

Eilat
New Commercial Centre
Tel. (059) 2268

Nahariya
Egged Bus Station, Shderot Gaaton
Tel. (04) 922126

Nazareth
Rehov Casanova
Tel. (065) 54144

Netanya
Kikar Haatzmaut
Tel. (053) 27286

Ramallah
Al Mughtaribin Square
Tel. (02) 953555/6

Tiberias
8 Rehov Alhadeff
Tel. (067) 20992

Zefat (Safed)
Municipality Building
Tel. (067) 30633

2.   **ISRAEL STUDENT TRAVEL
     ASSOCIATION (ISSTA)**

for good tours at low prices, International Student Identity Cards, and cheap overseas flights

Jerusalem
5 Rehov Eliasher
Tel. (02) 231418

Tel Aviv
109 Rehov Ben Yehuda
Tel. (03) 247164/5

Haifa
Beit Hakronot
Rehov Herzl
Tel (04) 669139

3. **ISRAEL INFORMATION CENTER**

   214 Rehov Yaffo
   Jerusalem

   for printed information on various aspects of Israel and Israeli society, from the government's view

4. **MINISTRY OF ABSORPTION**

   Rehov Ruppin
   Hakirya, Building 2
   Jerusalem
   Tel. (02) 61171

   for details about rights and programs for new immigrants, and details about coming to Israel to live

5. **TNUAT ALIYA**

   27 Rehov Abarbanel
   Building 4, Floor 4
   Jerusalem
   Tel. (02) 37504

   for how to keep alive the possibility of living in Israel when you're back where you came from

6. **TOUR VEALEH**

   17 Rehov Keren Hayesod
   Jerusalem
   Tel. (02) 233819

   for help in exploring the possibilities of living in Israel while you're visiting in Israel

7. **KIBBUTZ FEDERATION**

   Beit Mercaz Hakhaklai
   Tel Aviv
   Tel. (03) 250231

   for arranging stays of any length on kibbutz

8. **YOUTH AND HECHALUTZ**

   19a Rehov Keren Hayesod
   Jerusalem
   Tel. (02) 226111

   for programs in, and materials about, Israel; the best general address for such things

| 9. | MINISTRY OF INTERIOR | for extending and changing the status of visas once in Israel |

9. MINISTRY OF INTERIOR — for extending and changing the status of visas once in Israel

Jerusalem
Binyan Generali
Rehov Shlomzion Hamalka
Tel. (02) 221461

Tel Aviv
Migdal Shalom
9 Rehov Ahad Ha'am
Tel. (03) 51941

Haifa
Government Building
(across from Municipality)
Tel. (04) 64651

10. MOADON HA'OLEH — for information on living in Israel; the associations of new immigrants from English speaking countries have their offices there

9 Rehov Alkalai
Jerusalem

11. ISRAEL YOUTH HOSTELS ASSOCIATION — for information on youth hostels in Israel, and international youth hostel membership cards

3 Rehov Dorot Rishonim
Jerusalem
Tel. (02) 222073, 225925
P.O.Box 1075, Jerusalem

12. STUDENTS AUTHORITY — for information on programs of higher education in Israel open to foreign students, and assistance available to new immigrants studying in Israel

6 Rehov Hillel
Jerusalem
Tel. (02) 222371/2

13. PERSONAL ADDRESSES — for keeping track of how to get back to the people you meet, the places you go, the relatives you visit, etc.

Say Something !

WHEN YOU'RE FLYING

Welcome	Ba-ruch Ha-ba	ברוך הבא
Airplane	Ma-toss	מטוס
Pilot	Tay-yass	טייס
Steward	Da-yal	דייל
Stewardess	Da-yeh-let	דיילת
Airport	S'deh Te-oo-fah	שדה תעופה
Passport	Dar-kon	דרכון
Flight ticket	Kar-tiss Tis-a	כרטיס טיסה
Luggage	Miz-va-dah	מזוודה
Bag	Teek	תיק
Bon Voyage	De-rech Tzle-cha	דרך צלחה

AROUND YOU

Man	Ish	איש
Husband	Ba-al	בעל
Woman/wife	Ish-ah	אשה
Boy	Ye-led	ילד
Girl	Yal-dah	ילדה
House	Ba-yit	בית
Floor level	Ko-mah	קומה
Apartment	Di-rah	דירה
Street	Re-chov	רחוב
Town/city	Ir	עיר
Village	K'far	כפר
Collective settlement	Kib-butz	קבוץ
Country	Eh-retz	ארץ
Sky	Sha-ma-yeem	שמים
Sea	Yam	ים
Sun	She-mesh	שמש
Mountain	Har	הר
Valley	E-mek	עמק

WHAT'S THE TIME?

Time	Z'man	זמן
Minute	Re-ga	רגע
Hour	Sha-ah	שעה
Day	Yom	יום
Night	Lai-lah	לילה
Week	Sha-voo-a	שבוע
Month	Cho-desh	חודש
Year	Sha-nah	שנה
Today	Ha-yom	היום
Yesterday	Et-mol	אתמול
Tomorrow	Ma-char	מחר
What's the time?	Ma Ha-sha-ah?	מה השעה?
It's 1 o'clock	Ha-sha-ah E-hat	השעה אחת

181

Tell me when to get off	Ta-gid li ey-foh la-re-det	תגיד לי איפה לרדת
Forward	Ka-dee-mah	קדימה
Counsellor	Ma-drich/ah	מדריך/ה
Guide	Mo-reh/rah De-rech	מורה דרך
Group	K'vu-tzah	קבוצה

GREETINGS

Hello/Peace/Good-bye	Sha-lom	שלום
Good morning	Bo-ker Tov	בוקר טוב
Good evening	E-rev Tov	ערב טוב
Good night	Lai-lah Tov	לילה טוב
How are you?	Mah Sh'lom-cha/ech?	מה שלומך ?
Please/you're welcome	B'va-ka-shah	בבקשה
Excuse me	Sli-chah	סליחה
See you soon	L'hit-ra-ot	להתראות
Thank you	To-dah	תודה

SIMPLE WORDS

Yes	Ken	כן
No	Lo	לא
Maybe	Oo-lie	אולי
Of course	Be-tach	בטח
Good	Tov	טוב
Bad	Rah	רע
Where	Ey-foh	איפה
This/that	Zeh	זה
Who	Mi	מי
What	Mah	מה
Why	La-mah	למה
Do you have?	Yesh l'cha/lach?	יש לך ?

DOING THINGS

I am going	Ani ho-lech/et	אני הולך/ת
I am traveling	Ani no-seya/sa-at	אני נוסע/ת
I am drinking	Ani sho-teh/tah	אני שותה
I am writing	Ani ko-tev/et	אני כותב/ת
I am giving	Ani no-tain/tenet	אני נותן/ת
I am inquiring	Ani m'va-kesh/et	אני מבקש/ת
I am eating	Ani o-chel/et	אני אוכל/ת
I am taking	Ani lo-kayach/kachat	אני לוקח/ת
I see	Ani ro-eh/ah	אני שומע/ת
I hear	Ani sho-may-ah/ma-at	אני רוצה
I want	Ani ro-tzeh/tzah	

PLACES

Parliament	K'nes-set	כנסת
Cinema	Kol-no-a	קולנוע
Theatre	Tey-a-tron	תיאטרון
Museum	Mu-zay-ohn	מוזיאון
Synagogue	Beit K'nes-set	בית כנסת
Church	K'nei-si-yah	כנסיה

GETTING ALONG

Tourist	Ta-yar	תייר
Guest	O-re-ach	אורח
New Immigrant	Oleh/ah Cha-dash/a	עולה חדש(ה)
Hotel	Ma-lon	מלון
Room	Che-der	חדר
Dining Room	Cha-dar Ha-ochel	חדר האוכל
Waiter/ress	Mel-tzar/it	מלצר/ית
Meal	Aru-chah	ארוחה
Restaurant	Miss-a-dah	מסעדה
Water	Ma-yim	מים
Food	O-chel	אוכל
Table	Shul-chan	שולחן
Chair	Ki-sey	כסא
Ulpan	Ul-pan	אולפן
Book	Se-fer	ספר
Map	Ma-pah	מפה
Telephone	Te-li-fon	טלפון
Telephone token	A-si-mon	אסימון
Telegram	Miv-rak	מברק
Post office	Do-ar	דאר
Pen	Eyt	עט
Pencil	I-pa-ron	עפרון
Letter	Mich-tav	מכתב
Stamp	Bool	בול
Envelope	Ma-a-ta-fah	מעטפה
Aerogram	I-ge-ret A-vir	אגרת אוויר
Bathroom	She-ru-tim	שרותים
Youth Hostel	Ach-sa-ni-at No-ar	אכסנית נוער

BUYING AND TRAVELING

Sherut	She-rut	שרות
Taxi	Mo-neet	מונית
Car	Me-cho-neet	מכונית
Bus	O-to-boos	אוטובוס
Driver	Ne-hag	נהג
Train	Ra-ke-vet	רכבת
Ticket	Kar-tees	כרטיס
Road	K'vish	כביש
Money	Kes-sef	כסף
Gift	Ma-ta-nah	מתנה
Clothes	Be-ga-deem	לבוש
Earrings	A-gi-lim	עגילים
Ring	Ta-ba-at	טבעת
Shop/store	Cha-nut	חנות
Market	Shuk	שוק
Grocery Store	Ma-ko-let	מכולת
Receipt	Ka-ba-lah	קבלה
Central Bus Station	Ta-khana Mer-ka-zit	תחנה מרכזית
How much is this?	Ka-mah zeh o-leh?	כמה זה עולה?
Where is _____ street?	Ey-foh Re-chov _____?	איפה רחוב _____?
When is the next bus to...?	Ma-tai ha-o-to-boos ha-ba l	מתי האוטובוס הבא ל _____

183

Mosque	*Mis-gad*	מסגד
University	*Oo-ni-ver-see-ta*	אוניברסיטה

SECURITY WORDS

Help	*Ez-rah*	עזרה
Bomb	*P'tsa-tsah*	פצצה
Emergency	*Chey-room*	חרום
Shelter	*Mi-klat*	מקלט
Suspicious item	*Cha-fetz Cha-shood*	חפץ חשוד
Explosion	*Hit-po-ts'tsoot*	התפוצצות
Mine	*Mo-kesh*	מוקש
Danger	*Sa-ka-nah*	סכנה
Policeman/woman	*Sho-ter/et*	שוטר/ת

SICK?

Nurse	*A-chot*	אחות
Doctor	*Ro-feh/fah*	רופא
Infirmary	*Mir-pa-ah*	מרפאה
Examination	*B'di-kah*	בדיקה
Sick	*Cho-leh/ah*	חולה
Medicine	*T'ru-fah*	תרופה
Pill	*Ka-door*	כדור
Injection	*Z'ri-kah*	זריקה
Diarrhea	*Shil-shul*	שלשול

NUMBERS

One	*E-chad*	אחד
Two	*Shna-yim*	שניים
Three	*Shloh-shah*	שלשה
Four	*Ar-bah-ha*	ארבעה
Five	*Cha-mee-shah*	חמשה
Six	*Shee-shah*	ששה
Seven	*Shee-vah*	שבעה
Eight	*Shmoh-nah*	שמונה
Nine	*Tee-shah*	תשעה
Ten	*Assah-rah*	עשרה

ALSO Find out and write down the Hebrew words for all the things in your room and put signs on them. More than learning new words, you'll never forget where you left your bed or closet.

184

What Are You Doing?

The calendar on this page is to help you plan out what you'd like to do during the time you'll be in Israel. The following eight pages are for keeping a running account of what you actually end up doing when all your plans get changed around. And the "Blank Pages" section that follows is to give you the opportunity to explain it all.

Sun.	Mon.	Tues.	Wed.	Thurs.	Fri.	Shabbat

(If you're staying more than eight weeks, great, but you'll have to plan the rest of your visit elsewhere. Sorry.)

WHAT ARE YOU DOING?

	MORNING	AFTERNOON	EVENING
SUN			
MON			
TUES			
WED			
THURS			
FRI			
SHABBAT			

WHAT ARE YOU DOING?

	MORNING	AFTERNOON	EVENING
SUN			
MON			
TUES			
WED			
THURS			
FRI			
SHABBAT			

WHAT ARE YOU DOING?

	MORNING	AFTERNOON	EVENING
SUN			
MON			
TUES			
WED			
THURS			
FRI			
SHABBAT			

WHAT ARE YOU DOING?

	MORNING	AFTERNOON	EVENING
SUN			
MON			
TUES			
WED			
THURS			
FRI			
SHABBAT			

WHAT ARE YOU DOING?

	MORNING	AFTERNOON	EVENING
SUN			
MON			
TUES			
WED			
THURS			
FRI			
SHABBAT			

190

WHAT ARE YOU DOING?

	MORNING	AFTERNOON	EVENING
SUN			
MON			
TUES			
WED			
THURS			
FRI			
SHABBAT			

WHAT ARE YOU DOING?

	MORNING	AFTERNOON	EVENING
SUN			
MON			
TUES			
WED			
THURS			
FRI			
SHABBAT			

WHAT ARE YOU DOING?

	MORNING	AFTERNOON	EVENING
SUN			
MON			
TUES			
WED			
THURS			
FRI			
SHABBAT			

Blank Pages

We've left these pages for you to divide up and use as you want. Doodle, write, react, respond, contemplate, keep a diary, or whatever. (We only ask that you find something else on which to write home!) We know that everything that's happening to you is too amazing for words, but give it a try anyway!

Glossary

Hmmm . . . a glossary without entries. Very strange, but only temporary. There are a lot of terms in this book, both in English and Hebrew, with which you may not be familiar. Find out what they mean, and write up a glossary of your own.

Section 9
BACK "HOME"

ARRIVALS

CUSTOMS

DEPARTURES

ISRAEL

Back "Home"

Your time in Israel has ended; you're desperate. That burning love affair with Israel had but just begun, and now the two of you have been separated.

The intense desire to hold her earth close to you again.

The fierce drive to caress her lovely stones only once more.

The explosion in your heart to kiss that felafel a final time.

The throbbing need to sink slowly once again into that seat on the Egged bus.

Your mind won't stop wandering back to those ecstatic moments on the beach, the sun beating down on your back, the sound of waves soothing your head, and the *pushdakim* acting like @%+!$ all around you . . .

But snap out of that day dream. You're back. How does it feel?

1. ( ) weird
2. ( ) funny
3. ( ) fuzzy
4. ( ) discombobulated
5. ( ) normal

Don't be concerned. If you feel 1,2,3, or 4, you're more normal than if you feel normal. You're discovering culture shock in reverse. You expected everything to be strange when you went to Israel, but not when you returned to where you were brought up. Have you caught yourself . . .

( ) pushing your way onto a bus, instead of waiting nicely in line?

( ) bumping into someone and saying *slicha*?

( ) opening your bags for a security check when you walk into a store?

( ) going into McDonald's and ordering a felafel?

( ) cutting up tomatoes and cucumbers for breakfast?

( ) trying to hitch with your index finger down, and, as if that wasn't bad enough, explaining to curious people that you were waiting for a "tramp"?

( ) sending a letter to a friend on an Israeli aerogram?

( ) telling someone to meet you at Richie's Pizza?

( ) wondering why there's so much traffic on Shabbat?

( ) expecting the banks to be open on Sunday, or closed in the middle of the afternoon during the week?

( ) trying to feed a public telephone *assimonim*?

( ) bargaining for something in a store?

( ) bringing a canteen, hat, and camera everywhere you go?

( ) doing anything else ingenious?

Relax. We've been back to the Diaspora a few times ourselves, and we know the transition isn't easy. You have to get used to there being bigger cars, smaller money, and fewer camels. Readjusting means making the people and places you knew from before, familiar again. On the one hand, you may be feeling:

( ) enough was enough, and it's good to be back.

( ) there's no place like home.

( ) your friends who went to Europe had a better time.

( ) you're glad to finally have people other than Jews around you again.

But we'd more likely be better off asking if you're finding that:

( ) no one seems to understand what you've gone through?

( ) old friends and you just don't have all as much in common as you used to?

( ) being Jewish is something different than you'd thought it was?

( ) you're much more aware of Israel in the news now?

( ) your dog missed you?

231

( ) everyone wants to **know** about it, but no one really **cares** about it?

( ) you can't wait for that reunion?

( ) all of a sudden **you're** the Israel expert?

( ) you're already thinking about the next time?

( ) _____

Whatever, there's no need to despair. You'll be back some day, and in the meantime the relationship can continue to grow wherever you are. There are youth movements that understand what you're going through, with people who will talk to you and let you talk to them. People with whom you can commiserate, with whom you can share the experience, and with whom you can deepen your appreciation of Israel. People with whom you can dance the *hora*, sing *Hatikva*, create a discothèque Israeli style, share your pictures, eat felafel — the ultimate experience.

And if you don't want the people, there are all sorts of things available too: posters, printed materials, films, tapes, air-mail editions of Israeli papers to subscribe to, Israeli products to buy in stores, et cetera. Get in touch. Israel is as deeply attached to you, as you are to her. Your investment of emotion and energy has been too great to waste.

Offices geared toward your needs, and able to direct you elsewhere if necessary are:

AUSTRALIA
Youth and Hechalutz
Zionist Federation of Australia
and New Zealand
584 St. Kilda Road
Melbourne

ENGLAND
Jewish Agency
Rex House
4/12 Regent Street
London, S.W.1

SOUTH AFRICA
Youth Department
Zionist Center
84 DeVilliers Street
Johannesburg

CANADA
United Zionist Council
1247 Guy Street
Montreal, Quebec

UNITED STATES
American Zionist Youth Foundation
515 Park Avenue
New York, New York 10022

And if the organizations can't completely satisfy you, perhaps the following recipe can:

פלפל
Felafel

FELAFEL BALLS

1 16 ounce can of chick-peas,
   drained, **or**
2 cups cooked dried chick-peas
1 cup dried bread crumbs
1 egg, beaten
¼ cup finely chopped onion
2 cloves garlic, minced
2 tablespoons minced parsley
½ teaspoon salt
¼ teaspoon pepper

ACCESSORIES

pita bread
cabbage, chopped
tomatoes, diced
cucumber, diced
tahina sauce
oil for deep-frying

Mash chick-peas. Add all other felafel ball ingredients and mix well.
Shape batter into balls of approximately ½ inch diameter. Deep fry
for a few minutes until deep brown. Drain. Stuff into pita. Top with
mixture of vegetables. Pour on tahina sauce. Relive your Israel
experience. Recipe makes 15-20 balls — hardly enough to get
started!

234

Reading Into It ...

This is a list of a few basic books relating to Israel and the Jewish people — just some suggestions if you're looking for a place to start.

> None are poor except for those
> who lack knowledge
> —Pirke Avot

Bergman, Samuel. **Faith and Reason**. Washington, D.C.: B'nai B'rith Hillel Foundations. 1961 *(introductory collection of annotated excerpts from modern Jewish thought)*

Bettleheim, Bruno. **Children of the Dream**. N.Y.: Macmillan. 1969 *(very readable sociological study of kibbutz life)*

Collins, John & Lapierre, Dominique. **O Jerusalem**. N.Y.: Simon & Schuster. 1972 *(exciting journalistic account of the war between the Arabs and the Jews in the years 1947-8)*

Diamont, Max. **Jews, God, and History**. N.Y.: Signet Books. 1969 *(concise and readable history of the Jews throughout the centuries)*

Elon, Amos. **The Israelis: Founders and Sons**. N.Y.: Holt, Rinehart, & Winston. 1971 *(a critical look at Israeli society from the inside)*

Fox, Sarah. **Footloose in Jerusalem**. Jerusalem: The Center for Jewish Education in the Diaspora of Hebrew University. 1974. *(wonderful series of do-it-yourself walking tours through Jerusalem)*

Hertzberg, Arthur, ed. **The Zionist Idea**. N.Y.: Harper and Row. 1959 *(annotated collection of excerpts from classical Zionist thought)*

Heschel, A.J. **The Sabbath**. N.Y.: Harper & Row. 1966 *(a poetical expression of the meaning of Shabbat)*

Kurzman, Dan. **Genesis 1948**. N.Y.: World. 1970 *(novel-like historical account of Israel's struggle for independence)*

Laquer, Walter. **A History of Zionism**. London: Weidenfeld & Nicholson. 1972 *(advanced, in-depth history of the Jews' struggle for national liberation)*

Laquer, Walter. **The Israel-Arab Reader**. N.Y.: Bantam. 1970 *(annotated collection of primary sources documenting the development of the Israel-Arab conflict)*

Michener, James. **The Source.** N.Y.: A Fawcett Crest Book. 1965 *(historical novel of the Jewish people)*

Ministry of Information. **Facts About Israel** *(the title says it all)*

Postal, B. & Levy, W. **And the Hills Shouted for Joy.** N.Y.: David McKay Co, Inc. 1973 *(accounting of the events leading to Israel's independence)*

Shapira, Avraham, ed. **The Seventh Day.** London: Penguin. 1970 *(conversations of kibbutzniks on attitudes towards life in light of the Six Day War)*

Siegel, Strassfeld & Strassfeld. **The Jewish Catalog.** Philadelphia: Jewish Publication Society. 1973 *(contemporary do-it-yourself guide to Jewish living)*

Tsur, Muki. **What is Kibbutz?** N.Y.: American Zionist Youth Foundation. 1972 *(the kibbutz and its development in perspective)*

Uris, Leon. **Exodus.** N.Y.: Bantam. 1959 *(historical novel on the creation of the Jewish State)*

Vilnay, Zev. **The Guide to Israel.** *(it is what it says)*

Wiesel, Elie. **Night.** N.Y.: Hill and Wang. 1960 *(personal account of living through the Holocaust)*

Yadin, Yigael. **Massada.** London: Sphere Books. 1966 *(comprehensive review of Massada, viewed through the archaeological excavations carried out there by the author)*

He who meditates over words of Torah, finds ever new meaning in them.
—Rashi

FOUR EPILOGUES

A Parable

A traveling merchant was accustomed to carrying his wares from village to village on the back of a donkey. It was the only steady companion the man had in his wanderings, and naturally he became very fond of the animal. Not only did he depend on it for his living, but over the years he became very attached to it as a friend as well.

One day, as the old donkey was climbing to the top of a very high hill, it collapsed and died. The man was heartbroken. He took the animal to the side of the road, buried it, and, contemplating his fate, sat there and wept.

Two passers-by noticed the man in his grief and came to his side to find out what had happened. They saw the grave and asked, "A friend of yours?"

"A friend. Oh, what a friend," the man grieved. "I depended upon him for my very life. What was too heavy for me to bear, he would always take on his own back. And without ever a complaint, I tell you. Oh, how well he knew the ways of the world; when I would go astray he would always lead me back to the proper path. How will I ever be able to live without him?" The two travellers listened with compassion to the merchant's praises, tried to console him, and went on their way.

Said one to the other, "A truly righteous man lies buried there."

"Yes," nodded the other, "and without so much as even a simple gravestone over his head." The two determined to place a monument to the *tzadik* (צדיק – righteous man) over the grave, and went there regularly to tend it, using the time to search their own souls as they did so. Soon other people in the area, seeing these two there all the time, also began to come to the place to repent and meditate, and, as rumors of the power of the spot spread, people from far and wide would come there to pray and search their souls. In time an extravagant sanctuary was built over the grave and numerous people claimed it as their own holy spot.

Years later, the old merchant (who meanwhile knew nothing of all this) happened to be passing the spot on his travels again, having acquired a new donkey some time ago, and being quite satisfied with his lot. Gaping open-mouthed at what he saw before him, he recognized the two men who had comforted him on the top of this same hill so long ago. "What . . . what is all this?" he stammered in amazement.

"Your great and holy friend," they explained, "the *tzadik* you

buried here. We all come regularly to do him honor, and he in turn looks upon us in favor from his esteemed place in heaven."

The merchant broke out in uncontrollable laughter, "That righteous man, my dear friends, is nothing but a jackass."

Everyone rushed upon the merchant, incensed. They insisted that he retract his slander and demanded an explanation. He, of course, could only tell them the truth. They, of course, refused to believe him. And so enraged did they become that they hanged him on that very spot and went on worshipping.

Be careful about accepting everything here as perfect just because it's Israel. We still don't know on what hill the donkey's buried. But also be careful in your criticism. Not only is the truth sometimes subjective, but there are many genuinely righteous men buried here too.

239

To Build And To Plant

We live at Neve Ilan now, a communal settlement high in the middle of the country. Stand with us there for a few minutes. To the east, watch the Judean foothills stretching towards Jerusalem. Turn around, and see the Shalom Tower rising starkly above Tel Aviv. And begin to appreciate that there is more than 63 kilometers separating them. One city still throbs with an ancient culture, even as it labors to accommodate contemporary society; the other was but born today, and struggles now in search of a past. And it is our generation that must bridge this vast expanse of time and values.

Biblical prophecy promised our return, and pioneers of our time have turned the vision into reality. But the physical existence of a Jewish entity was never conceived of as sufficient; there has always been as well the intention to make of it a society responsive to our heritage.

By now you have come to understand how this dream itself rests on our ancient traditions, spiritual values, and living symbols being deeply rooted in our forefathers' affinity to the Land of Israel. Now you can begin to explain it to others, to help bring all of this Jewishness into the lives of today's Jews: not to plunge Israel back into the days of the Bible, but rather to cause the messages of the Bible to permeate the consciousness of contemporary Jewry.

No, all of this is not aimed directly at securing the physical safety

240

of the State of Israel, but nevertheless it has its own *chalutzic* spirit; for there is an entire cultural and spiritual frontier of *Yisrael* still to be developed and guarded.

For so long homeless, the Jewish people has quite suddenly and ill-preparedly been thrust into a situation of statehood. And so perhaps we must come to look at ourselves as in a severe state of "nation-shock." With our leaders practically learning how to build a state only after it came into being, it is no wonder Israel has its difficulties; the wonder is that we have achieved so much. Those with the luxuries of time and space separating them from the turmoil of society building here, are afforded the opportunity to equip themselves advantageously for the challenge of entering into a partnership with the fledgling state and its inhabitants, based on understanding and vision — regardless of where they are to live.

We are the first generation in two millenia for whom faith alone has not had to suffice; for us there is the fact of Israel. We are the ones, through no effort of our own, to witness the fulfillment of a 2000 year old pledge:

> "Behold, the days come, saith the Lord, that I will sow the house of Israel and the house of Judah with the seed of man, and with the seed of beast. And it shall come to pass that . . ., as I have watched over them to pluck up and to break down, and to overthrow and to destroy, and to afflict; so will I watch over them to build and to plant . . ." *(Jeremiah 31:27-8)*

The Land, the People, and the Book; inextricably intertwined. We are all part of it. But what part is it ours to play?

Look back and forth again. It is a long way between ancient Jerusalem and modern Tel Aviv, isn't it? What does it mean to be among those who return — even in a spiritual sense — *"to build and to plant"*?

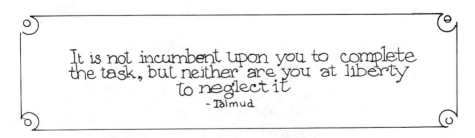

It is not incumbent upon you to complete the task, but neither are you at liberty to neglect it
— Talmud

Think about it, and write an epilogue of your own.

An Epilogue Of Your Own

What is your Israel really all about? Let your mind wander for a while, over — expectations... past... present... future... change... belonging... longing... having... doing...

בשנה הבאה
Bashana Haba'ah

Bashana haba'ah,
Neishev al hamirpeset
V'nispor tziporim nod'dot

Y'ladim b'chufsha
Y'sachaku tofeset
Bein habayit l'vein hasadot

Od tir'eh, od tir'eh
Kama tov yihiyeh
Bashana bashana haba'ah
2

Anavim adumim
Yav'shilu ad ha'erev
V'yug'shu tson'nim lashulchan

V'ruchot r'dumim
Yis'u el eim haderech
Itonim y'shanim v'anan

Od tir'eh . . .

Bashana haba'ah
Nifros kapot yadayim
Mul ha'or hanigar halavan

Anafa l'vana
Tfros ka'or k'nafayim
V'hashemesh tizrach b'tochan

בשנה הבאה
נשב על המרפסת
ונספור צפורים נודדות

ילדים בחופשה
ישחקו תופסת
בין הבית לבין השדות

עוד תראה עוד תראה
כמה טוב יהיה
בשנה בשנה הבאה.
2

ענבים אדומים
יבשילו עד הערב
ויוגשו צוננים לשולחן.

ורוחות רדומים
ישאו אל אם הדרך
עתונים ישנים וענן

עוד תראה . . .

בשנה הבאה
נפרוש כפות ידיים
מול האור הניגר הלבן

אנפה לבנה
תפרוש כאור כנפיים
והשמש תזרח בתוכן

NEXT YEAR

Next year
We'll sit on the porch
And count migrating birds

Children on vacation
Will play tag
Between the house and the fields.

Chorus : You will yet see, you will yet see
How good it will be
Next year.

Red grapes
Will ripen till the evening
And will be served chilled to the table.

And languid winds
Will carry to the crossroads
Old newspapers and a cloud.

Next year
We will spread out our hands
Towards the radiant light.

A white heron
Like a light will spread her wings
And within them the sun will rise.

—Ehud Manor
© by April Music Ltd.

Answers And Notes

SCRAMBLES

p.14: grapefruit/olives/figs/grapes/apples//**felafel**
p.38: land/people/Bible/spirit//**Israel**
p.72: Tzahal/Shabbat/Torah/Negev/Diaspora//**Theodor Herzl**

CROSSWORD   The Everything Israel — p 17

CRYPTO—QUOTES   pp.44—46

1. When thou eatest the labour of thy hands, happy shalt thou be, and it shall be well with thee. — Psalms 128:2

2. When you will return to nature . . . you will know that you have returned to yourself, that when you hid from nature, you hid from yourself. — A.D. Gordon

3. If a sapling were in your hand and you were told that the Messiah had come, first plant the sapling, then go and greet him. — Rabbi Yochanan Ben Zakai

4. A man's life is sustained by trees. Just as others have planted for you, plant for the sake of your children. — Yalkut Shimoni

5. And the tree of the field shall yield its fruit and the earth shall yield her produce and they shall be safe in their land and they shall know that I am the Lord. — Ezekiel 34:27

CRYPTO—GRAM

pp. 92 - 97

ERETZ ISRAEL IS NOT
SOMETHING APART FROM
THE SOUL OF THE JEW-
ISH PEOPLE. IT IS
MERE NATIONAL POS-
SESSION, SERVING AS
A MEANS OF UNIFYING
OUR PEOPLE AND BUT-
TRESSING ITS MATERI-
AL OR EVEN ITS SPI-
RITUAL, SURVIVAL
ERETZ ISRAEL IS PART
OF THE VERY ESSENCE
OF OUR NATIONHOOD
IT IS BOUND ORGANI-
CALLY TO ITS VERY
LIFE AND INNER BEING
— RAV KOOK (1865-1935)

246

NOTES

1. The specific references in this article to the origins of the symbol of the State of Israel are based on: Nogah Hareuveni, **The Menorah and the Olive Branch** *(filmstrip and text)* (Kiryat Ono: Neot Kedumim, Ltd.) 1971. The theme of the connection between the Land, the People, and the Book, which runs throughout this volume, owes much to Nogah's personal inspiration.

2. The references in this article to the origins of the symbols of the holidays and the phenomena of ecological concern in Jewish texts are based on: Nogah Hareuveni, **Pesach** *(filmstrip and text)* (Kiryat Ono: Neot Kedumum, Ltd.) 1971, and Hareuveni, **Ecology in the Bible** *(filmstrip and text)* (Kiryat Ono: Neot Kedumim, Ltd.) 1971.

3. Based on an episode in: Miklos Nyiszli, **Auschwitz** (Greenwich: Fawcett Publications) 1960, pp.88-92.

4. Based on an account in: Dan Kurzman, **Genesis 1948** (N.Y.: New American Library) 1970, pp.326-327. With permission of the publisher.

5. Based on: Nogah Hareuveni, **Sabbath** *(filmstrip and text)* (Kiryat Ono: Neot Kedumim, Ltd.) 1971.

6. Based on an account in: Bernard Postal and Henry Levy, **And the Hills Shouted for Joy** (N.Y.: David McKay Co., Inc.) 1973, p.262. With permission of the publisher.

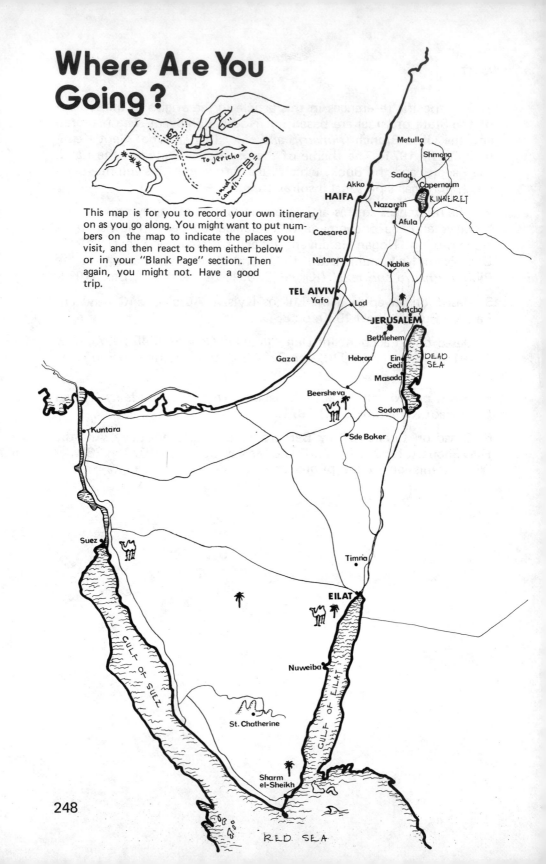

Where Are You Going?

This map is for you to record your own itinerary on as you go along. You might want to put numbers on the map to indicate the places you visit, and then react to them either below or in your "Blank Page" section. Then again, you might not. Have a good trip.

248